PORT OUT STARBOAR

The Diary of
Rachel A. Sheringham
1901 - 1905

Edited by Ian Newton

S.S. ASIA

PORT OUT STARBOARD HOME

The Diary of Rachel A. Sheringham
1901 - 1905

Edited by Ian Newton

Published by Margaret Newton
3 Brickfield Cottages, Roughton Road,
Cromer, Norfolk NR27 0HL

First printed September 1991

Printed by Studioprint
23 Charles Wood Road, Dereham, Norfolk NR19 1SX

ISBN No. 0 9518228 0 2

Preface

RACHEL ANNA GARLAND
married first
William George Sheringham
and their children were:
Margaret, Geoffrey, Olive, Alice, Gertrude, Maria, Helen

Arthur William Sheringham
married first
Annette Packenham-Walsh
and their children were:
Georgina, Arthur, Harold, Kathleen, Anthony Ilex

On April 20th, 1897 Rachel Anna Sheringham (nee Garland)
married Arthur William Sheringham
Their children were:
Ruth, born February 22nd, 1898. Rachel, born June 7th, 1900

At the opening of the diary the ages of the members of the family most often mentioned in it were as follows: Rachel Anna, 43; Arthur, 57, Georgina, 21; Arthur (junior) 20; Geoffrey, 19; Helen, 12; Anthony Ilex, 10; Ruth, 3; Rachel "Baby", 11 months.

Rachel A. Sheringham by VanDyk Norwich

Introduction

The diary came to light following the death of Ruth Sheringham (Ruthie in the diary) in 1979 when her effects were sold at auction. Inadvertently the diary was also sold, being at the bottom of a box of magazines. It came into my husband's possession a year or so later, given him by a friend who knew of his family's long association with India. Several more years elapsed before I rediscovered it among our books. I had not read it before, in its entirety, and on doing so I became curious to know more of the writer. Even when I had read the diary I knew tantalisingly little about her other than the name of several of the children of the family, her name and that of her husband. It was not in my mind, at that time, to publish the diary, only to satisfy my curiosity. On re-reading the diary several more times my curiosity became something more than that, I began to nurture the hope that I might find one of the two small children, Ruth or Rachel, who figure so much in the pages of the diary, still living. At that time, of course, I could not have known that both were dead.

My quest began at the public library in Holt where I received encouragement and advice on how to proceed with a task which was an entirely new experience for me. The staff at the Norwich City Library set me on a trail which was to lead to a meeting with David Sheringham who, although not a descendent of the writer of the diary, is, as far as I have ascertained so far, the only living male descendent of her husband, Colonel Arthur William Sheringham. To David Sheringham I am indebted in so many ways, for the generous loan of all but two of the photographs used here as illustrations, for information on the family and, most particularly, for his enthusiastic support for the idea that the diary be published. He freely admitted that, had the diary been in his possession (as indeed it might have been) he would never have found the time to prepare it for publication himself.

I should also like to thank the following people. Keith Skipper of Radio Norfolk (for his encouragement and generous radio time), Ethel Levell and her daughter in law Elsie (who were instrumental in arranging an introduction to David Sheringham), Muriel Cross (whose best friends at school were Ruth and Rachel), Mr and Mrs Neville Hopking, Maurice Woods, President of the Shipdham Society and his wife (who kindly made available the water colour painting made by Rachel Anna Sheringham of the bungalow at Singhur), Mr and Mrs G.H. Groves (of the Shipdham Society) and Charles A. Drake (a churchwarden of the Holy Cross Church at Caston).

Margaret Newton

Cromer, 1991

Excerpts from a diary kept by Rachel A. Sheringham and begun on 1st May, 1901.

MAY 1 Bought this book in Liverpool this morning with the intention of making a short daily record. Ilex came from Parkgate before we had finished breakfast for one more day with Ruth. Arthur and I are to dine with Mr and Mrs Blood this evening.

MAY 2 We had a very pleasant evening with our kind friends who have also been good enough to say Ilex is to go to them for a few days. I am writing this at 8 p.m. having been on board the Asia since about 4 p.m. We have three very roomy cabins which will make the voyage easier for us. The babies are lying happily feet together in a lower berth and nurse will sleep opposite them on a bench. There are only three other passengers, a youngish lady going to Port Said and a lady very much like Mrs Sandford only considerably bigger with a very dark friend or relative. The crew and stewards are coloured. We had dinner at 6 o'clock p.m. a wholesome meal but not to be compared with the menu of the White Stars or Cunarders. Arthur has had a great deal of trouble with the hounds, the Railway Company having delayed getting them onto the ship until past five o'clock though they left Hanwell last night and arrived at Birkenhead before 7 a.m. today. They are in huge kennels with iron bars in front, some holding five and others four. As I write at 8.20 p.m. the shouting of the native crew and hauling of chains and ropes is accompanied by the gradual passing of lights and a "floaty" feeling which tells me we are leaving the loading berth and saying goodbye to England. I feel more at home on a boat than I did when I last sailed from the old country which was four years ago also in May but I do not like the smell or general surroundings of a boat any better than I did then.

MAY 3 It has been a delightfully fine day with a calm sea but this evening it is a bit chilly and there is a bit of a swell which makes both nurse and me a bit qualmish. The children slept well and have been perfectly happy all day sleeping and feeding as though in their ordinary nursery life. Arthur has spent nearly the whole day with the hounds, he was out soon after 4 a.m. for tea and tub before 8.30 breakfast. At 10 I went to help him to feed them which was a lengthy business for only one kennel at a time could be attended to and the natives who were

Nurse with Ruth left Baby right

supposed to help were of very little use except to fetch the biscuit from the big tub in which it had been soaked over night. I find both the lady passengers are missionaries, the younger one going to work in Cairo. the elder with her adopted dark son to some part of India. 8.30, now going to bed glad to have got through at least one day of sea life.

MAY 5 I was too seedy all yesterday to make any effort to write; I found myself unable to sit at the dinner table the night before, and after a night of real "pitch and toss", for though the sea looked calm there was a horrid swell on, I awoke with less energy than any worm. Ruth, too, was a bit seedy and after dressing we tried to lie on deck rolled in all the warm clothing, eiderdowns and fur cloak included that we could muster, however a quarter of an hour was enough and Ruth said she didn't want to go "lickety rockety" and was immediately ill so we crawled down-stairs to my cabin and both went to sleep. Ruth awoke quite refreshed and by 4 o'clock was quite lively again. I spent the whole day fasting and dozing and tumbled into bed about 8 o'clock. This morning (Margie's 20th birthday) found me rather better and I have gradually improved. The day has been beautifully bright but not very warm. The swell has decreased since we got further into the bay. I am told we shall see the coast of Portugal tomorrow morning. The last remnant of land was the Tuskar lighthouse raised from the isolated rock on which it stands, it is somewhere off the south of Ireland and we passed it about 4 p.m. on May 3rd. On account of the fog, guns were firing at stated intervals from the lighthouse and the captain seemed a bit anxious until we were safely past. The hounds employ Arthur nearly the whole of every day, he goes to them each morning at 4 a.m. spending about three hours with them, then directly after breakfast he goes to them feeding, exercising and petting them until lunch, between lunch and tea he lets them run loose, about seven or eight couples at a time and has a final inspection after dinner.

MAY 6 My "sea legs" are sprouting at last I am glad to say and in spite of a very rolling night I felt pretty well when I dressed and I ventured into the saloon for breakfast. We are having today what the captain calls the Portuguese Trade Wind and I don't like it at all for it is very cold and the sea is decidedly rough, there is some likelihood of shipping seas on the forward deck in which case the kennels will all have to be lashed onto the hatches again, they were put there at first but it was so hard to get at them there and the sea was so calm that the captain most good naturedly had them all moved onto the deck the second day, they are comfortably lashed to the bulwarks on either side of the ship making what the old Scotch captain calls "The Curral's Village". We are through the bay and I expected to have seen the coast of Portugal this morning but no such pleasant sight as land has met my eye, the sea is beautiful, the deepest blue with feathery white crests, but so treacherous looking I detest it. I am being very lazy at present having done nothing but a few stitches of knitting besides reading one of the books I am taking out for Captain Lyle Smyth "A Subaltern's letters to his wife" which gives a most interesting account of S. Africa its manners and customs and especially that side of the war as seen from "Rivington's Guides" of whom the writer was one.

MAY 7 Georgie's birthday, many happy returns to her. We had a very rough night and the poor hounds must have suffered a good deal for they had many seas over their deck. They are now moved back on to the hatches where they will keep dry but it gives the "master" an enormous lot of trouble and he is so energetic and thorough that he gets quite tired out by dinner time. We saw land this morning as soon as we got up and were off the Portuguese coast until about 10 o'clock, we saw numbers of biggish steamers homeward bound and a pretty fleet of trawlers off Lisbon looking as Ruth very sagely remarked "just like birdies". She has a little cold and is not quite herself today but baby is full of go and is bursting with health and energy. I am told we shall probably pass "Gib" about 4 o'clock p.m. tomorrow. This is a very slow boat and we shall very likely take 30 days to get to Bombay, she carries an enormous cargo worth £300,000, chiefly whisky and beer but also iron rails and engine fittings. I am much better today and have eaten quite well. The food is good but is not prepared nor served with much refinement and the table manners of our fellow feeders do not conduce to appetite made fastidious already by the ship and its surroundings.

MAY 8 About 8 o'clock last night we passed Cape St Vincent and early this morning saw land on both sides of us this growing clearer as we neared it made the morning pass with considerable interest, the weather has been perfect, a calm deep blue sea, brilliant sun and lovely breeze being with us all day. We could see houses distantly with the naked eye both on the African and Spanish coasts and the hills with their grassy slopes and sandy or rocky prominences interspersed made lovely landscapes. About 5 p.m. the unmistakable form of "Gib" appeared, looking like a gigantic rock standing alone in the middle of the sea. On closer investigation one could see the low lying ground with which it is connected with the mainland. At 6 o'clock we passed it so closely that we could see the flag flying from a mast in a signal house. I thought at once of all those at home who will be glad to see in tomorrow's papers that the S.S. Asia passed Gibralter on May 8. We had been just five days and 20 hours at sea. We have now to settle down to another whole week of sea for we shall probably only see Malta in the dim distance between this and Port Said. Ruth's cold is better and she is quite good tempered again, baby now has a little cold which makes her rather fretful and the sun and sea air have made her cheeks redder than ever, both children seem to enjoy sea life.

MAY 9 The snow capped peaks of Sierra Nevada greeted us on rising today and until about midday the coast of Spain was well in view. The day was fine but not very warm and in the middle of the afternoon a stiffish breeze got up which caused an uncomfortable suggestion of reeling and writhing, gradually it increased until the ship pitched and soon the other two lady passengers and nurse were prostrate, beyond having a headache and feeling very giddy I did not suffer. The voyage has now gone back into horrid monotony, the captain says that if this wind continues (which impedes our already slow progress) he will have to put into Malta for coals as there will not be enough to last until we reach Port Said, but as the ship would only stay there an hour at most the little stop would be more tantalizing than pleasurable.

MAY 10 A bright sunny day but such wind, very cold and very blustering making it impossible to sit on deck and very unpleasant to walk.

MAY 11 At a quarter to six a.m. Arthur awoke me to look at a water spout. It was a funny looking object, not at all like the illustrations I have seen, there was a dense black cloud with part of it forming a sort of bag like an inverted bee hive from the middle of which hung what looked like a rope reaching nearly to the sea where it was met by a sort of misty foam. It must have been a good many miles away for it was not very distinct even through glasses. About eight o'clock we had a heavy rain and hail shower and during the day there have been frequent squalls. The boat has pitched and rolled badly and I have spent most of the day in my berth.

MAY 12 After a night of many storms, wind, rain, hail, thunder and lightning we have much better weather today, we passed the little island of Zembra about eight a.m. and later rounded Cape Bon. With a fair wind and smooth sea we are making a better run. At three p.m. we pass the island of Pantelleria, a rather comfortable cosy looking place with numbers of white houses dotted over its flattish sides and a lighthouse perched conspicuously over its highest point. On closer view it discloses carefully cultivated fields arranged in terraces and enclosed by fences almost up to the hill tops and quite down to the water's edge. I am told it is a very productive island and given up to vine culture. Once an Italian penal settlement, now the property of the Duke of Sparta.

MAY 13 Arthur called me up a little before six a.m. to catch a glimpse of Malta which looked bright and cheery with its white buildings and green fields but we only had a distant view (I think we were about five miles off) for the coal held out better than the captain anticipated and he was very glad to go straight on to Port Said. A beautiful sunny day but still not warm enough to sit on deck which would have been nice with the sea perfectly calm as it was.

MAY 14 Baby was very restless all night and neither nurse nor I could get much sleep. At early tea time (six a.m.) Arthur came in enveloped in his waterproof cloak, told me it was a beastly morning, sea running very high, bitterly cold wind and drenching rain. the hounds were very wet and miserable and were showing signs of colds and cough. The kennels have now been covered with tarpaulins and the poor beasts seem thankful for the shelter. The captain and the officers are extremely kind in arranging everything they possibly can for their welfare.

MAY 16 After midday on the 14th, when I last wrote, until this morning I have been altogether out of the running, the sea grew rougher and rougher making the boat pitch more and more heavily both day and night. She shipped so much water that the engines had to be slowed down to half speed and yesterday we made the miserable run of 109 miles in 24 hours, even the stewardess was ill and Ruth being the only one amongst us who could move, even Arthur said it was all he could do to walk from one end of the ship to the other. This morning it was delightful to wake feeling that at least one's bed was not flying from beneath one and the gradual assurance that there was a calm sea made me only too glad to be up and dressed, so that I am now actually writing in the saloon before breakfast. It was said that we should reach Port Said early tomorrow but I expect the rough weather of the last two days will have caused further delay. Baby has been very poorly since the night of the 13th, sick and feverish with great irritation in her gums and ears, she began to improve last night and after a hot bath followed by a good night's rest is much brighter this morning.

MAY 17 A bright windy day, the boat rolling a good deal but as there is no pitching it is bearable.

MAY 18 At 5.30 a.m. Arthur came and told me Port Said was in sight, so I lost no time in getting up and by the time I was dressed the town was well in view. About 8.30 a smart little steam launch came bustling alongside and in a very few minutes the pilot coming in a small rowing boat from the launch jumped, after climbing the rope ladder on our ship's side, on board the Asia. About half an hour later we were anchored in the harbour opposite our coaling wharf. At the entrance of the harbour there is a gigantic stone statue of Monsieur de Lesseps. The ship was hardly anchored before she was invaded by Egyptians with their wares for sale, Maltese lace, sponges, picture postcards, cigarettes, Turkish delight, embroideries, nougat. As Arthur and I were going ashore we withstood all temptations to spend money, my propensities are fortunately for the family under strict control for I have no money at all and Arthur has only a few shillings for he gave all he had into the Purser's keeping as soon as we left England. At 9.30 a.m. we were rowed ashore by two Arabs in a small boat whose name "Jerusalem" was roughly painted in green and red in rude English characters. I wish I could give a clear description of my first

Georgina eldest daughter of Colonel A.W. Sheringham

impressions of an Eastern town, with its curious flat topped, flat sided houses, the windows covered with quaint wooden shutters, something between Moorish and Venetian, and sometimes by tatters. Crowds of chattering Arabs with their long blue gowns and turbanned heads, red fezzed Egyptians of all degree from some smart looking gunners of the Khedive's army in faultless khaki uniforms with very new looking leather belts and leggings, to comparative beggars, everywhere the same red fez, sometimes blackened almost beyond recognition it is true and sometimes as worn by officials, such as river police looking bright and most becoming to the faces, generally handsome, of those who wore them. Well, we wandered on through crowds of foreigners to the beach where I picked up some familiar looking shells, "knives and forks", "fan shells" and others such as I have found on the many home sands where I have wandered. There was a happy looking family party, father, mother, two girls and three little children, sitting happily chatting and looking on the beach in the most ordinary everyday summer seaside clothing, in fact I could almost fancy myself on the Wells beach except that no green grass or scrub was visible. From the beach we found our way to the Post Office, a French one, and having bought stamps posted our letters home. Then on through strange streets with stranger shops of a rather low class description interspersed with cafes or restaurants of sorts where one saw Egyptians with hubble bubbles, Arabs, French, Italians, in fact representatives of all nations, with coffee, iced drinks or refreshments of some sort or other, some playing dominoes others cards, all looking happy and energetic. Then we passed a number of quiet looking nuns with Red Cross badges on their arms. Then sitting at a street corner a group of lazy, dirty Arab women with the lower parts of their faces covered and the string of somethings, whether of metal or wood I cannot say, hanging as frontals before their eyes; how I do wish I could draw! Then again we walked on and passed a real modern railway station with rows of patient horses standing in their carriages, sort of ramshackle Victorias waiting outside for passengers. On through a miniature desert where were groups of sleeping men and donkeys, then back and into a small enclosure intended, I suppose, as a recreation ground, the thick coarse grass having some sort of life kept in it by vigorous watering from a hose, a band stand in the middle the base of which composed of rocks and stones was standing in sluggish looking water, all the nooks and crannies being filled with maiden hair and palm ferns growing luxuriantly in their unpromising looking surroundings. Down the principal street where some really good shops, stationers, drapers, chemists, hairdressers, jewellers and confectioners exposed many tempting things for sale. Having spent about three hours ashore we took another little boat and again rowed across the little bay to our floating whilom home. The Canal Company's offices are very prominent close to the edge of the bay with broad white steps leading from a well kept garden in front down to the water. The building is of white stone with three large domes either with green marble a palish bright shade, or some natural tinted stone, several storeys high and with innumerable windows in straight lines right across in many rows from end to end. We found various letters awaiting us on board but none of any interest. Luncheon over I amused myself watching the process of coaling. Huge barges were moored each side of us and to and from their dusky depths weird looking black objects ran as hard as they could leg it carrying each one a full basket up and an empty one down the shaky slanting planks. Huge busy ants they seemed, coal begrimed Arabs though they were. From 9.30 a.m. till 2.30 p.m. the toil went on unceasingly and in those five hours 550 tons of coal were stowed away for our use during the rest of the voyage. About 4.30 p.m. up bustled another steam launch and on board her came another pilot for us, this time to take us through the canal; moorings unfastened we began gliding slowly and almost noiselessly away and within a few minutes we were in the canal. I well remember in my school days at Bognor what pains my good old governess Miss Chamberlain took to describe the wonderful engineering feat which I think was at that time in progress and how the name of Lesseps always faded from my memory whenever I wished to show how much interested I was in my lesson of geography, now after 26 years I am learning the wonders of it all with comparative ease. I only wish my own school girls were here to learn it too. Well, I can't say much by way of description for a canal is a canal, here for many miles after leaving Port Said on one side which I will call the

Arabian side, in fact I think for the whole length of the canal there is nothing to be seen but vast stretches of sand, with sand hills and sand holes and sand mountains and still more sand, away and away. On the Egyptian side however there is a pleasant stretch of green for many miles, rushes, trees and palms all growing into one another along the bank. Every now and then at stated intervals there is a telegraph station and at each spot there is a happy looking tidy house with garden shewing cool green feathery trees and brilliant flowers. All along at the back of the bank there is a fresh water canal which comes from the Nile to supply Port Said and this keeps the vegetable growth green and fresh looking. We saw a marvellous sunset, the sand giving back such strange reflections that at one time the sun looked like a gigantic globe of copper set upon a huge pedestal of the same dazzling metal. Darkness quickly set in after sunset and the sky, changed to deepest bluey green, soon sparkled.

Each pilot takes with him a small boat, a couple of men and a powerful dynamo. The latter is fixed to the bows of the ship and the boat is slung with its occupants amidships. We soon found out what these were all wanted for, for a strong light ahead from a similar dynamo to ours and a signal from the bank told us to "tie up" for the passing of the coming ship, it seemed but a few seconds before the little boat was lowered and the men had fixed the heavy hawsers fore and aft to piles in the bank and we waited while a strange ship glided slowly past. Then after shipping the hawsers on we went for about half an hour when another signal stopped us, this time there were three lights seen one behind another the farthest being about five miles away and the captain and the pilot decided that it would be wiser to wait until all three ships had passed. I waited on deck until 9 o'clock, having seen two of the number pass and then went to bed thoroughly tired after a most interesting and enjoyable day.

I find I have not mentioned weather which however had been perfect all day. We found it a little hot on shore but Arthur with his helmet and I with a green lined white umbrella felt no inconvenience and directly we were back on the boat we had a lovely breeze.

MAY 19 Sunday. At 6 this morning Arthur told me we had already passed the big salt lakes which are about half way in the canal and also

Ismailia, which could be seen in the distance. As I was dressing we passed a French boat with a number of troops from Madagascar. This time the other boat tied up and we went on. By 8 o'clock Suez was well in view though the city proper stands too far away from the canal to be clearly seen without glasses. Then we came to the newer part, a sort of suburb with nice looking houses and plenty of palms at the side of the canal. The clock from a handsome looking R.C. Church struck eight and then the home like sound of church bells reminded us that we were beginning our third Sunday at sea. The pilot now left in a steam launch which called for him and we anchored in a shallow bay before starting for the last and shorter part of our voyage. We had more letters brought to us during breakfast, amongst them one from Arthur T, really intended for Harold.

After breakfast we found there were seven deck passengers who had joined the ship bound for Bombay. Four were Arabs and two women, the latter Italian Jewesses I am told. These passengers have no cabin accommodation and no food supplied by the ship, nothing but water and their passage for which they pay £3.10.00. The women are well dressed (or rather were) in fashionable European clothes and brought with them various trunks and packages. Directly they were on board they slipped off their outer clothing and wrapped themselves in loose cotton gowns. In these they are lying half asleep on coloured rugs or cushions. They are some source of interest but although we can go where we like on the main deck where they are it will not be so pleasant as when we had it to ourselves. Ruth's swing is hung there and there is greater length for her to run up and down but the upper deck which has now a double awning is delightfully shady and this is of course exclusively for 1st Class passengers' use. I have written from May 17. today so I have accomplished a good many pages of scribbling and now at 3.30 p.m. we are steaming down the Red Sea with a lovely breeze and hardly a ripple on the water. Huge ranges of sand mountains visible both on the Egyptian and Arabian coasts.

MAY 10 A day in the Red Sea. Land was to be seen for a short time on the Arabian coast then nothing but sea which, contradicting its name, was as blue as any part of the Mediterranean. I got up at 6 and mended a blouse on deck before breakfast. During lunch we passed two small islands known as "The Brothers" both looking like big brown loaves with their straight sides and flat tops. There is a lighthouse on the larger one and a pretty hot time of it the caretakers must have. All their food supplies and water are brought in boats from Lower Egypt. It was a decidedly hot day but a lovely breeze which came at any rate onto the upper deck made that part of the ship quite comfortable and I spent most of the day working, quite the most industrious one I have had since coming on board, there was hardly any motion and the sea made only a splashing which sounded cool.

MAY 21 There was an extremely heavy dew last night and the decks were as wet as though it had been raining heavily. The cabins had been so very hot all night I was glad to escape so went up soon after 5 o'clock in my dressing gown and sat in the little smoking room on the upper deck with doors and window open. I am writing this before breakfast and we expect a very hot day.

MAY 22 Very hot but made bearable by a slight breeze, intensely hot as light, went and sat on deck where Mrs Warren and "Eddie" had been sleeping soon after 4 a.m. Sea all day of oily calmness.

MAY 23 Another intensely hot night, about 3.45 Arthur came and advised me to go on deck where he said it was fairly cool. It was quite dark and several indistinct humps and lumps on deck shewed where our fellow travellers were sleeping. Arthur and I rolled ourselves up on deck chairs and had a little snooze before the sun rise. The children sleep well both night and day and do not seem inconvenienced by the heat though it shews itself in the "prickly" form all over baby's face and head and a good deal on Ruth's neck. The captain says we shall be out of the Red Sea tomorrow night and already is every now and then a little coolness in the air coming from the South which tells of the ocean beyond.

MAY 24 The heat at night was worse than before, Arthur did not try to sleep in his cabin. I made an effort as my bed was moved onto the upper berth just beneath the port but it was so intolerably stuffy I carried my pillows up and spent the rest of the night in a chair on deck. We passed numerous islands during the day, bare and bleak looking. The children are smothered with prickly heat but make very little trouble of it.

MAY 25 Last night we all slept outside, nurse and baby on the main deck just outside their cabin, Arthur Ruth and I in a row on the upper deck. The night was very close and airless and I did not sleep much. I missed Ruth in the middle of the night and looking round saw her lying fast asleep on the bare deck some distance from her bed. I don't know how long she had been there but Arthur put her back to bed as soon as we found her. We passed several islands again yesterday, one called Jebel Zukur the principal of the Hanish Group was clearly seen through the glasses. There have been three vessels totally wrecked round this island during the last 20 years and the masts are visible above the water. The islands are not inhabited but are visited occasionally by Arab pirates who are always on the look out for ships in distress. There are many dangerous coral reefs in this part of the Red Sea and the old captain took a somewhat longer course than most ships to avoid all dangers. During the night between 12 and 1 o'clock we passed Perim Island, the harbour lights shone out brightly and that from the lighthouse towered above the rest and was visible for about 20 miles.

This morning, about 9 a.m., we passed Aden, the place itself lies far back in a bay so we could only see the buildings on the outskirts, but the whole district looks bare and uninteresting in the extreme, black rocks of enormous height and glaring sand looking fiercely hot beneath the blazing sun.

We are now fairly out of the Red Sea and I am glad to say for the heat though not amounting to the infernal height or depth that I expected from all accounts has been sufficiently uncomfortable and when out of the Gulf of Aden we hope to have the rest of the voyage moderately cool.

MAY 26 Another very hot night. The breeze which had been fairly fresh all day dropped about 9 p.m. We slept on deck as last night. We shall not be into the Arabian Sea before tonight as we are going so slowly, the usual speed of the ship is only 9 knots an hour and we have been going considerably less, owing it is said to the foul condition of the ship's bottom. It ought to have been in dry dock for scraping and cleaning when last at home but owing to the delay already caused by the Marseilles strike the owners postponed the cleaning till she gets to Bombay and we are delayed in consequence. Saw numbers of flying fish.

MAY 27 Arthur and I had our beds moved onto the hatch over the saloon last night, leaving Ruth on the lower deck with nurse. We had a really good night's rest as there was a lovely breeze blowing straight on us. It was disappointing to have an intensely hot day afterwards and the discomfort of the heat was greatly exaggerated by the pitching and rolling of the ship for as soon as the Gulf of Aden was passed we found a big swell in the Arabian Sea. I felt a regular worm the whole day and could do nothing but doze.

MAY 28 Last night was extremely hot and no breeze came to cool us though we again slept on the hatch. We are longing for the end of the voyage which we hope will be early next Sunday June 2nd.

MAY 29 A cooler day with a very smooth sea. The ship is now making better running so we shall probably get into Bombay on Saturday night.

MAY 30 The day a trifle cooler, but hot at night.

MAY 31 The same record, both day and night as yesterday but we know now we shall get into Bombay some time tomorrow.

JUNE 1 This morning we are seeing various ships, we have seen none since we left Aden, hundreds of flying fish and a few birds have been the only life to be seen except that on board our own ship. About 3 o'clock we met the P. and O. with homeward mails so I am sorry I cannot post the many letters I have written until next week.

Very soon after this we sighted land and from this time things have become more and more interesting. Numbers of dhows and small craft of all sorts gradually came in view and soon, that is to say about 5 o'clock, (I am writing this several days later so cannot remember times accurately) the pilot's brig was seen coming towards us and we were steering for the harbour at Bombay. Numbers of cocoa nut trees growing close to the water's edge gave the refreshing green look that we have been longing for. Passed Colaber lighthouse, then another. Saw Malabar Hill with houses and buildings dotted thickly all over it and went slowly on until we were stopped by signal and anchored in the open. I hardly know whether to call it sea, bay, or harbour. Gradually lights appeared on boats, ships and on shore.

DECEMBER 1901 Fancy having left this poor diary in such an abrupt

Poona July 1902
Ruth aged 4 with dog called Rachel!
Rachel aged 2 with dog called Ruth!

way just six months ago; time is peculiar in this country, it has a way of slipping away in oily, indolent fashion, leaving very little afterwards to shew. I know I have been incessantly busy ever since I arrived but I have nothing to produce as a result of six months hard labour. To return to June 1st, where I left off my daily record so suddenly, I can now only give a very scrappy account of what we have done since that time.

It was so late on the evening of June 1st when we got into dock that we were obliged to sleep there, at least to lie down in night attire for what with the heat, mosquitoes and smells and noises of the dock there is very little sleep to be had. About 11 o'clock next day, being Sunday, we took our farewells of the Asia and her officers and made our way to the station, nurse, the children and I in a carriage of sorts, Arthur in a dog cart with Mr. Birkett, a member of the Bombay Hunt who kindly came to help with the hounds, and then a long procession of 17 bullock waggons carrying kennels containing hounds, luggage and sacks of Spratts dog biscuits. We had about an hour to wait at the station, nurse and the children resting in a comfortable waiting room, Arthur making various arrangements for the journey to Poona and I prowling around and amusing myself with the novel sights everywhere before me. The native patter, families with wives and children and bundles galore, squatting all about the large open space with their perpetual, monotonous chatter and picturesque Eastern dress especially attracted my attention.

We were fortunate in having a carriage to ourselves for the journey and the children being tucked up on broad seats were soon soundly asleep and remained so for more than half the journey. After travelling for about an hour over more or less flat and rather marshy ground we began to ascend the ghats, the train slowly climbing a zig zag path through innumerable tunnels. The scenery is very grand at all times but just at the end of the hot dry season it is perhaps less beautiful than at any time of the year. When I went over the same ground again in October, just after the rains the waterfalls and masses of maidenhair and other ferns added very much to the beauty.

Arriving at Poona between 6 and 7 p.m. we were met by Mrs Pinney who took us to the house which she had most kindly prepared for us, and we all did justice to the first meal which by Mrs Pinney's thoughtful care had been provided.

I cannot go into detailed account of our time in Poona from now until October 1st except to say that we met with great kindness on all sides and received dozens of invitations for dances, dinners, luncheons, at home and every sort of function, a few of which we accepted and enjoyed the entertainments. The Governor and Lady Northcote were particularly kind and from them we also received many invitations. On one occasion Arthur and I, with hounds and horses, stayed at Government House for the night having previously dined there with about half a dozen other regular members of the Hunt ready for a lawn meet next morning.

Ruth enjoyed a children's party kindly given by Lady Northcote and I was especially interested at a "purdah" party, also given by her, where I had an opportunity of seeing dozens of native ladies in their gala dress and adorned with masses of exquisite jewels.

On October 1st, by the kind invitation of Mr Armstrong, one of Arthur's staunchest supporters in the hunting field, our whole menage went to Dapuri where the hounds and horses no less than ourselves enjoyed his hospitality for a fortnight. Hunting meanwhile was done from this centre by which means another part of the country was available for sport.

On October 15th Arthur and I were entertained at the ghymkhana by members of the Poona and Kirkee Hunt. Many kind and flattering things were said of Arthur and his management of the hunting which he was asked and has promised to undertake again next season. Then the President, Surgeon General Price, handed him a silver cigar box and me a silver smelling bottle, both of which are engraved with our names, dates etc.

The next day we left Dapuri and returned to Poona where for nearly a week we were the guests of Colonel Bull whose kindness and hospitality were unbounded. Then, for a fortnight, we lived in a big, almost empty, house next to the kennels for many of the hounds, being at the time unsold, Arthur would not leave them though we had engaged a house at Singhur from October 15th.

I have said very little about hounds and hunting which really are the chief interest to us both, because of the speculation involved, but, thanks to Arthur's untiring energy and incessant care, hunting throughout the season has been excellent giving the greatest satisfaction to the entire hunting community and hounds have stood the season well, a few deaths only have occurred from accident and disease.

On November 7th we migrated to Singhur with children and 13 couple of hounds belonging to us.

The air and freedom of the life on this hill suits us all exactly. The children are able to run about bare footed nearly all day and Arthur and I find plenty of resources, both apart and in company. Friends come and see us from time to time. Mr and Mrs Keatinge were our first visitors a day or two after our arrival. Colonel and Mrs Hallett, about a fortnight later, then a signalling party came to the hill for a few days practice and we saw two young subalterns, who were in charge, very frequently.

December 15th is a day I make special note of because of a remarkable walk Arthur and I took. We started by a little hill path intending to go round from one gate to the other on the opposite side of the hill but walking some distance after the sun grew hot and Arthur having remembered seeing some natives come up the hillside by a short cut we decided we would do the same. At first the difficulties were nothing but those of an ordinary steep climb up a very narrow path. The higher we got, however, the steeper and more difficult it became. The short dry grass afforded no foothold and we found it impossible to go in boots so, one at a time, we sat upon the only firm looking rock and, taking off our boots, we left them there. The path became worse and we could only ascend on hands and knees. Arthur, who was of course leading, was cutting little steps with his pocket knife. Every now and then we came to a piece of almost upright bare rock and how we climbed these places we hardly know. However, to retrace our steps was impossible and we went perseveringly but, I must confess, very nervously on. The last 8 or 10 feet was a mass of almost perpendicular rock and as by this time my hands and knees were getting very shaky I felt quite unable to tackle it. I managed to find a fairly firm foothold and also clung with both hands to the rock above and determined to wait there. I felt very doubtful whether Arthur would reach the top safely. However he did manage it and then lost no time in calling for help and getting a strong rope which was lowered to me. After putting it around me under my arms I was delighted to be hauled safely to the top.

Captain Lyle-Smyth came to us for a Christmas visit. We had a very pleasant week while he was with us making several excursions for shooting to the valleys below and taking breakfast with us.

1902 to 1903

S.S. ASIA

JAN 8. 1902 The nurse who came out with us left on December 2nd and I was fortunate in getting a nice woman as a stop gap. She stayed a month until I found a permanent help.

Today Mrs Keatinge and her baby arrived for a visit. The three children enjoyed playing together and her companionship is very pleasant. We spend our mornings at needlework on the verandah and do nothing more tiring than taking a longish walk in the evening. We have two tents pitched at the foot of the hill and when our visitors leave we are going to take the children and camp there for several days. Arthur has already been several times for one night and has shot each time some splendid young peafowl which are capital eating, very much like turkeys and quite as big.

JAN 19 Mr and Mrs Keatinge and family left.

JAN 28 Arthur, children, nurse and I went to camp at the foot of the hill.

FEB 2 Returned to hill after five most enjoyable days below.

FEB 20 Arthur, with hounds, horses, syces and dog boy went to camp at Akawadi.

FEB 24 Arthur spent day in Poona.

FEB 28 Arthur and hounds returned to hill.

MAR 16 Mr Johnston and Arthur went to foot of hill with hounds. Arthur stayed the night in tent end returned early the next morning.

MAR 19 Mr Johnston came again for one night intending to shoot a panther which prowls around. After making great preparations to stay out all night he told us next morning he was too sleepy to stay out after 11 p.m. He was much annoyed on going to examine the ground to find the brute's footmarks all over the place near where he had been placed and could not forgive himself for not having waited longer.

MAR 26 Big fire on hill below.

MAR 27 Festival of Hooli going on. A native "tamasha" outside the garden gave me and the children vast amusement.

MAR 28 Thunder and many clouds. Afterwards a nice shower of rain lasting for about 20 minutes beginning about 6 p.m. Except for a few drops in January one evening this is the first rain there has been since last October. Another tamasha.

MAR 29 Good Friday. A heavier shower than yesterday began

Water colour painted by Rachel Ann Sheringham of the bungalow Singhur 1905

considerably sooner. Much distant thunder.

MAR 31 Feast of Sivaji by Rajah of Sitara.

APR 6 Arthur went to Poona for Bombay to fetch more hounds.

APR 9 Arthur returned.

APR 17 Mr. Armstrong came.

APR 20 Our wedding day. Started at 4.30 a.m., rode down the hill. After riding down to the lake we found a jack which hounds were able to hunt a short time. Spent the day under some big mangoes. Rode up and got home soon after 7 p.m.

APR 21 Arthur's birthday.

APR 23 Mr Armstrong left.

APR 24 Arthur and I started at 5 a.m. and took hounds to Kundenpoor. Found and ran a jack. Found fox, ran him for ten minutes and killed in the open.

MAY 2 Arthur with hounds started at 5 a.m., rode to Donji. I walked down half an hour later, horse met me at foot of the hill and I rode to meet him. Spent day under trees, returned riding, at 7 p.m.

MAY 4 Heavy thunder and slight rain during afternoon.

MAY 17 Saturday. Arthur went to Poona, taking hounds and horses; started by moonlight at 8 p.m.

MAY 29 Very heavy rain (after much thunder and lightning from 4 p.m.) fell at 6 p.m. for about an hour and again during the night.

MAY 30 Arthur arrived soon after 5 a.m. having travelled from Poona through the night in a bullock wagon. Heavy rain as yesterday. Arthur left at 8 p.m. walking down the hill with coolie and a lantern to return to Poona in the same uncomfortable way that he came.

JUNE 2 Storms, mists and rain drive insects to shelter. Tons of fleas and a few B.flats coming into the house decides me to leave on the 5th instead of the 7th as first arranged with Arthur.

JUNE 5 After three days of packing and general settling and putting to rights we make our descent. 54 coolies carrying kit, children and puppies, some of the latter which were big enough to walk being led down by a dog boy. We left the house at 3 p.m. punctually, Dora and I walking by the side of the children who thought it great fun to be each hoisted astride the shoulders of a coolie. We reached the foot of the hill in less than an hour and finding the hound cart ready for its canine passengers and a comfortable landau and pair of ponies which Arthur had sent for us we left soon after 4 p.m. for Poona.

We began by having a good meal of bread, butter, hard eggs, plantains, tea and milk which I had brought for us and I had had nothing since breakfast and the children had only a little Bovril at mid-day. After being well refreshed we were all amused to watch people and things as we went along and we gradually got into the busy, bustling life of Poona which seemed at first a somewhat violent contrast to our quiet hill life. We arrived at 10, more than an hour before I had told Arthur to expect us consequently he was not in the house to welcome us as he intended. But the house itself was a charming surprise for it is a delightful one, large airy, well arranged and spotlessly clean, my good old husband having personally supervised the cleaning of the house throughout as well as of the furniture which shone with a brilliant polish.

JUNE 6 Between 9 and 10 a.m. good Colonel Bull came to pay his salaams and give us welcome; he said the children were "simply splendid".

JUNE 7 Heavy and persistent rain nearly all day. We were very lucky to have come on the 5th which was quite fine. This was the day (June 7th) I had at first arranged to come.

JUNE 8 Arthur and I lunched with Colonel Bull.

JUNE 13 A busy week has passed very quickly and my delightful house is beginning to look quite a finished home. The monsoon has broken in earnest and we have had great quantities of rain, but the children have such ample room for exercise and play indoors that they are jolly and good tempered in spite of not getting out very much. Arthur gets up at 4 a.m. twice a week and 5 a.m. other mornings. I have not ridden with him yet but hope to go early next week. He gets back to breakfast about midday and we have a good feed being breakfast and lunch combined.

JULY Poona season as usual, endless dinners, dances, at homes, luncheons. Captain and Mrs Marden joined us late in July, first as visitors, afterwards sharing house expenses.

SEPT Very good hunting season which ended last day of September when we gave a big picnic breakfast under the trees near Pashau Lake.

Hunt dinner given at the Gymkhana in our honour on October 4th, a great number of men and women present. Sir R. Low took me in and made an excellent speech, full of praise for Arthur's management, a new "Soutar" saddle was afterwards presented to Arthur and a gold fox head safety pin brooch to me.

OCT 7 Returned to Singhur, just a month earlier than last year. Very unsettled weather on and off till the second week in November, rain and mist very frequently with cold winds at night. several young hounds died from pneumonia in consequence.

Colonel and Mrs Channer spent a week with us at the end of October. Mrs Lester, a native infantry officer's wife, took a neighbouring bungalow for a month leaving towards the end of November. I found her a pleasant, bright companion.

NOV: Mr Creaghe and Mr Stowell arrived about 10 a.m. Sunday having come from Dapuri to spend a day with us which we much enjoyed.

NOV 27 Arthur and I were to have joined Colonel Bull and some friends at Kadakwasla for breakfast at 11.30 a.m. but during the night I had been aroused by hearing Ruthie shouting "Ayah". As the calling went on I went to see what was the matter and found the children quite alone. Arthur and the servants got up and went out with the lanterns searching without success in every likely place. By day light another search was made in wider directions but at present no trace has been found. Her box, dhurrie (cover) are left but as her blanket and chatty (earthen water pot) are gone I suppose her flight was premeditated. She had been grumbling a good deal the last fortnight. Arthur spent the day at Kadakwasla but said he was nowhere without his mate! So did not very much enjoy it.

NOV 30 We expected the Marden family today for a five days visit which they had themselves proposed but when I had made every preparation, both for house and food arrangements, they changed their minds and are not coming. I have plenty of occupation with entire charge of the children added to needle-work with "reeling writhing and drawling!" (vide Alice in Wonderland) as recreations.

I had just got as far as (writing) this when the boy came and told me three chairs with "sahib log" were coming up the hill, and almost at the same time a note was given to me. This proved to be from Captain

Marden saying that they were coming after all and it should have reached me last night. As it was I hardly finished reading it when the "sahib log in the chairs" were in view and turned out to be Captain and Mrs Marden, baby, English nurse and ayah which, although a most agreeable surprise in one way, was disconcerting as I had all the curtains removed from the bungalow which I had prepared for them. They only stayed two days as Mrs Marden found the wind too high for the baby and they were bothered by "creeping things" in the bungalow.

DEC 2 Geoffrey arrived looking remarkably fit. The Marden family left.

DEC 6 Geoffrey and Arthur spent a long day in the valley. Weather here most uncomfortable, high winds and very cold until 10 a.m., then rain, later thick mist and heavy rain.

DEC 7 Thick mist. Arthur is wearing his thickest English suit and the children their flannel dressing gowns outside their clothes, as well as warm socks and shoes; they and Geoffrey have bad colds. I have many warm underclothes with blue serge coat and skirt.

DEC 8 Geoffrey left soon after 7 a.m. Thick fog.

DEC 9 Thick fog which cleared twice during the day for a few minutes only. Rain at night.

DEC 10 Thick mist again but warmer. Heavy rain from 3 p.m. onwards. I forgot to say the missing ayah wrote calmly, after six days absence, requesting me to forward her belongings as she had safely arrived at her home after a somewhat uncomfortable journey!

DEC 11 Rain continued most of the night and fog this morning, denser than ever. It cleared about 2.30 p.m. and I took Ruthie for a walk round the hill, the first time she had been out for 6 days. Children were able to go out again after tea. Slight drizzle began a little before 6 p.m. More fog, high wind, almighty rain.

DEC 12 Clearer in early morning but again foggy by 8.30., things getting very damp and musty in the house. Got fine by 10 a.m. and remained fairly clear all day. Towards evening the sky became much less cloudy and by 6.30 the moon rose with a nice cheery look in her face. At bed time the night was beautifully clear with a brilliant moon.

DEC 13 Such a relief to have a bright sunny morning. Found a nice lot of mushrooms for breakfast. I am having every door and window throughout the house opened wide to let in sun and fresh air and so get rid of the damp clammy feeling which has hung about the house during the last week. Heavy clouds in the morning. Finding mushrooms again.

DEC 14 Too disappointing! To find the hill again enveloped in mist at 6 a.m., got fairly clear by 8.30 but clouds occasionally hang low on the hill and when clear enough to see below we notice mist lying densely over the lake and all along the rivers. Rode early this morning, have not done so for a fortnight owing to weather, ayah's sudden departure and various other things. After riding I picked mushrooms for an hour. Am beginning to want more exercise. About 5 p.m. we watched rain clouds coming gradually along the valleys, the sound of pouring rain getting gradually nearer and more distinct. No rain fell here but lightning and distant thunder went on throughout the evening.

Dec 15 A nice clear morning and I rode again. Weather fine until about 3 p.m. after which showers, more or less heavy, continued to fall for the rest of the day.

DEC 16 Arthur went shooting with Captain Marden. a fine day.

DEC 17 Mist in early morning. Clear afterwards. Rain at 5 p.m. for an hour and again this evening and at night.

DEC 18 Alternate mist and sunshine throughout morning. Hot. Heavy rain at night.

DEC 19 Went to Arvi with Arthur and started at 7 a.m. Got back at 5.30 p.m. Fine day. Big fair at Kundanpur. Bought lota (brass pot) and toys for children. I found the air quite different on our return, fresh and clear.

DEC 20 Lovely morning - fine all day.

DEC 23 Long walk with Arthur around fort before breakfast.

DEC 24 Rode to Arvi, back a new way across lovely downs. Started 7 a.m., back at 11 a.m. Weather glorious since the 19th.

DEC 25 Christmas Day. Full of joy for the children who have heaps of presents from Poona and from England.

1903 to 1904

S.S. ASIA

JAN 1st 1903 We had a small ox killed to commemorate the Coronation of King Edward Vll, the Delhi Durbar and all festivities in this connection taking place on this day throughout India.
Great excitement all day trying to get a panther which had been seen by a coolie coming up from Kalyan to his day's work. We soon saw the beast from the fort wall, quietly prowling about below but he quickly discovered he was being watched and began to crouch in low grass and hide under bushes. Arthur, having no rifle, extracted the shot from some cartridges and refilled them with bullets found amongst the old "cave" ammunition and as soon as a party of beaters could be collected he took up a position. Unfortunately the panther, after exposing himself several times, took refuge under some huge rocks before he could be driven within range of the gun and from this place the natives tried every means of driving him out without success. Arthur had taken up another position just above the cave and the natives lighted a fire, hoping to smoke the beast out, but though Arthur waited and watched for three hours expecting the beast to make a rush, nothing appeared. The natives were so certain the panther had not left that they began digging and continued until darkness was gathering. Early next morning they continued and about 9 a.m. came upon the panther's dead body, evidently suffocated by the strategy.
He was a smallish beast, 5ft 5 ins from nose to tip of tail but very handsomely marked. I wanted Arthur to let me buy the skin but as he had had no part in killing him he wouldn't let me. The natives therefore slung him on a pole and carried him off with the intention of getting the usual government reward from the Collector in Poona. When they reached Kadakwasla, however, they sold him to a sahib who wished for the skin.
I sent this account to the Poona paper, as my weekly contribution, but not at once so that it did not appear in print at once. Meanwhile, two different men in Poona had been saying that they had just shot a panther near Singhur! Captain Marden wrote and told me that my paragraph caused considerable consternation in Poona when it appeared - Honesty is the best Policy!
JAN 4 All went off to Arvi as soon as we had had chota hazri (early light breakfast) tents having been forwarded the day before, such a

cavalcade. Arthur and baby on one horse, Ruth and I on another, a syce (groom) on a third. There followed 2 syces walking, 22 hounds and 2 dog boys, cook, ayah and 2 table servants besides 28 coolies carrying kit for human, canine and equine comforts.

Had a very pleasant week in camp. Arthur did a lot of shooting and kept us more than supplied with deer, hare, quail and pigeons. Hounds also did plenty of work hunting daily.

JAN 10 All returned to Singhur.

JAN 21 Arthur, horses and hounds went to Arvi and stayed the night.

JAN 22 Arthur came back in the evening bringing a deer, 3 hares, 2 quail and a pigeon.

JAN 25 My birthday started with Arthur at 6.30 a.m. Spent the day in Arvi valley, returned after tea, Arthur staying the night in tent left from our former camp.

JAN 29 Got up at 4.30 a.m. Arthur and I walked down the steep path by light of a lantern having two horses led behind. On reaching the foot Arthur went off to try and shoot peafowl and I rode off to Kadakwasla. There a syce with horse and cart, having gone forward the day before, was waiting for me and I drove on to Poona reaching the Marden's house about 9.15 a.m.

Spent two days pleasantly with them, going on the river the first afternoon and to the Gymkhana the next. I saw very few people I knew, numbers of changes having occurred since October.

JAN 31 Drove to foot of riding road where Arthur had sent a horse to meet me, the syce, by his orders, having boiled water ready to make a cup of tea for me directly I arrived. I reached the top of the hill about 10.40 having left the Marden's house at 7.5 a.m. found Arthur and the children on the look out and got warmly greeted on my return.

FEB 12 Arthur with hounds and horses went to Arvi for a few days in camp returning on the 15th.

FEB 21 Baby covered with brilliant red rash; she is not ill but has been fretful and unlike herself for several days. Kept her in bed.

FEB 22 Ruthie's 5th birthday. Baby better but I kept her in bed most of the day because the rash is still out. Ruthie and I walked as far as the cave on the riding path after chota hazri and in it she soon discovered a hare which we managed to keep from escaping until

Alms for a beggar at Poona
Baby, Beggar, Ruth

Arthur and the hounds came by, he then sent for bullets and his gun; he couldn't shoot himself owing to a crippled hand so he took Ruth home on his pony and I stayed with the hare till the butler arrived. He shot it very soon after he arrived on the scene.

We are always delighted to live by the "sweat of the brow" and Ruth's lucky birthday find saved, or rather prolonged, the life of one of our tame ducks which we contemplated killing for dinner today.

MAR 5 A day's mountaineering. Arthur and I started walking a little after 7 a.m. taking 4 coolies to explore a distant range of hills. Walked and climbed, often over very "jumpy" places until 12 when we reached the peak we had hoped to arrive at for breakfast. A large peepul tree and a nest of big milk bushes gave welcome shade and as we had been told we found about half a dozen tanks cut in the rock at the extreme summit. One of them held a quantity of icy cold water. After breakfast we dawdled and surveyed the surrounding country until 2 p.m. then began our descent to the Kalyan Valley where our horses had been sent to meet us. I saw below, near, a well under shade and then rode home reaching the house about 6.15 p.m. after a delightful 12 hours outing.

We had bad luck in the way of shooting. We saw two huge boars, a very large deer and several hares, but not one within shot so had to content ourselves with pigeon.

MAR 10 Long day down by Kadakwasla Lake, glorious day with nice fresh breeze. Had a longish walk to try and get some peafowl. Arthur got two and we then went back for breakfast at 12 o'clock under thick trees bearing very sweet scented blossoms close by the edge of the lake. The beauty of everything around made me long for home, children and friends to share our enjoyment. After feeding ourselves, hounds and horses and "lazing" for a time, we took another long walk through bogs this time, after snipe. Arthur quite cock awhoop at slaughtering 14 1/2 couple - every one that got up.

MAR 12 Arthur with hounds and horses went to camp at Arvi. Morning began with a cold, thick mist, just like those we had in November. Clear by 9 o'clock. First day of a great Hindu feast; numbers came to visit the temple.

MAR 13 Great tamasha of drums, etc. outside during tea. Just as I was going to have my tub, before dinner, a voice outside the door said "May I come in?". It proved to be Mr Creaghe who had come over from Dapuri to stay till Monday. The letter he had sent two days before to say he was coming had not turned up. It was rather tiresome, his arriving so late and unexpectedly, with Arthur away. However, I managed to find a bed, table, chair and bath which I put into the cottage and he "shook down" all right . I had him on my hands all the next day for though I sent word to Arthur to say he was here I wrote at the same time to say that I was very short of food. He did not come back till early a day later, then bringing 3 hares and 3 pigeons.

MAR 15 Arthur came back at 8.30 a.m. bringing tents and all camp things which had been out at Arvi since we went in January.

MAR 16 Mr Creaghe left. Many villagers came to make tamasha but we had to stop them as it became an expensive matter to give so many rupees. Some rather good wrestling was done by native youths, their wiry brown limbs intertwining like writhing snakes as they tried to throw each other.

MAR 20 Hindu feast as last year, which I called "Feast of Sivaji" (see March 31 - 02). I find by having read some Mahratta History it is a feast given every year to Brahmins, Mahrattas and poor Hindus within a certain radius. The feast is given outside the principal temple here which was built on the spot where Ram Rajah, younger son of Sivaji died. He left funds for its yearly continuance on the anniversary of his death and the arrangements are made by the ruling Rajah of Satara.

MAR 25 Big hill fires have been going on for three days and nights until the surrounding country is now quite black and desolate looking. We watched the fires below the fort last night for some time, the glare of them quite lighting up the hill and the roar and crackling of the fire as it lapped up mile after mile of long grass and undergrowth could be heard at a great distance.

Major England paid us a flying visit yesterday; he bicycled from Poona to the foot of the hill, walked up and reached us in time for breakfast at 10.30 a.m. and left us soon after 12 o'clock to walk down the hill and bicycle back to Poona where he had an engagement at 3 p.m.

APR 1 Mr Armstrong arrived just as we were going to breakfast and spent the day with us.

APR 3 Another nice day down by the lake in our usual picnic place. After two long shoots, with breakfast in between, we determined, about 3 p.m., to have a swim in the lake. My objections to having neither towels nor bathing dress were quickly over-ruled by Arthur whose great forte in this country is making use of things under his hand. Accordingly, with a serviette each for a towel and a table cloth and safety pins to form a bathing dress for me!! off we went. We found a very retired place and had a most lovely swim in very deep water just warm enough to prevent any feeling of chill and returned to our shady place at 4 p.m. for tea.

APR 4 8 a.m. I was just in the midst of writing yesterday's outing when Arthur came in carrying Ruth in his arms saying, "I don't know if she is hurt, she has just tumbled into a cave." Beyond some scratches and grazes on face, hands and arms, and a bit of shaking, I think she is all right but it has given us all a great fright. I have just been to look at the place. the tank is about 30 feet deep and has an inch or two of mud and water at the bottom, the water which reached nearly to the top six months ago having been used for the garden. There is a ledge of rock protruding at a depth of about 12 feet where Ruth fell and on this she luckily caught . Arthur, who was getting lettuces in the garden, heard a dull thump followed by falling stones and was horrified to find the child had fallen. She is so very venturesome we have been fearing some sort of accident to her for a long time and I trust this will teach her to be more careful.

APR 4 Arthur went to Poona to say good-bye to Colonel Bull, starting about 6 a.m. and returning about 6 p.m.

At 9.30 a.m. the Armstrong family arrived and, at the same time, a strange man walked up the hill, he proved to be Colonel Jooks whom I recognised, although I had only once spoken to him in Poona. I asked him to join us for breakfast. So we were a big party and our tiny room was well filled with five grown ups and three children. The last three days have been extremely hot, I do not remember any such heat here last year.

APR 5 Arthur and I started at 4 p.m. to ride to Karakwasla where we joined Mr Keatinge who was in the Engineers' bungalow there. We had a pleasant sail on the lake before dinner, though there was not much breeze. Stayed the night and started for home the next morning at 7 bringing Mr Keatinge with us. He stayed three days.

APR 15 Thunder and a hail storm followed by a nice refreshing rain for about an hour cleared the air and we had considerably cooler air for the next 36 hours. However, it soon began to warm up again.

APR 18 Major England came, stayed the night and left the following evening.

APR 20 Wedding Day.

APR 21 Being Arthur's birthday, he and I did a long day out.Got up at 5 a.m., rode down the hill, had a very long walk round spur above Akawadi but though we saw heaps of game had only one chance of a shot. A peafowl was wounded with broken wing but through coolies' want of energy the bird got away. Had breakfast in a mango grove at 11.30 and rested for two hours. Then walked again and shot pigeon, quail and doves for the "pot".

APR 23 Arthur and I rode to Khed Shivapur and spent the day with Mr Keatinge whose camp is now there.

MAY 6 Colonel Channer came, leaving on the 9th.

From this time till May 15th my time was spent very industriously in packing and sorting, not only for my journey but for Arthur as I was anxious to leave everything in good order for him. We had a long day out together on the hills on the 14th and arranged a picnic tea at a certain spot, our children, the Armstrong family and Mr and Mrs Duxbury meeting us at 5 p.m. About 4 p.m. on the 14th we sent off all the luggage which had not been already dispatched, also the old ayah and the 2nd boy, Shiwa, as we wanted them to be ready awaiting us in Poona.

I went the round of the bungalows with the children during the evening to say "good-bye" to the various hill visitors and after putting them to bed we had dinner and soon retired ourselves for the order "chota hazri at 3 sharp tomorrow morning" had been given to the butler.

MAY 15 Got up at 3 a.m. Dressed the chicks and after having chota hazri and sending the little ones down the hill on the backs of coolies, under the care of two syces and Mr Duxbury, who chanced to be going early to Poona and had promised to take Ruthie in his tonga (a light, two wheeled vehicle), Arthur and I rode down the hill. At the foot of the bridle path baby was awaiting us in the cart as we had arranged and we heard that Ruthie had already started for Poona. We sent back the saddle horses with a syce and had a pleasant cool drive to Poona reaching the Bratty's house about 8 a.m. where a second, and most welcome chota hazri of tea, toast and fruit, was ready spread in the verandah.

Ruthie had safely arrived before us and was going a round of stables, kennels, poultry yard, etc., when we arrived. The children had baths and a lovely sleep left with the ayah while Arthur and I went and did various business in Poona. After looking at various cottages I was delighted that Arthur eventually decided to take rooms for three or four months at the Poona Hotel, for in this way he is saved all the trouble of house keeping and is sure of pleasant society when he wants it while he can enjoy solitude to his heart's content in his own quarters if he prefers for he has bed room, sitting room, dressing room and bathroom.

We got back for breakfast at 10.30 a.m. having done only part of our work and directly afterwards went out again for the rest, gladly returning as soon as we had finished for baths and a little rest for the heat of Poona was very great. After tea Mrs Bratty took me for a drive with dinner at 7.30. Almost immediately afterwards we went to the station.

We had engaged a Second Class compartment and were thus able to get comfortably settled into it whilst in a siding and had only to be coupled to the mail train on its arrival.

It was an awfully hot night and in spite of regularly undressing neither Arthur nor I could get much rest, the children, however, slept fairly well. On reaching Bombay the following morning Arthur and I rushed to the various waiting rooms for a wash and I managed to have a most refreshing splash in a huge marble bath in an infinitesimal space of time. The children washed and brushed, we all did justice to a comfortable chota hazri in the station refreshment room. Arthur having, meanwhile, sent Shiwa off to the dock with the luggage.

We followed at our leisure and after first seeing the captain of the Britannia and my cabin we left the children on board under Shiwa's care while we went to Bankers, Ship Agents,shops and all sorts of

places, getting back to the ship about 11.30.
We said good bye almost at once as it was awfully hot in dock and we (the passengers) had to wait about to be inspected by a plague doctor and then go straight on board, none but passengers being allowed on after the inspection. Arthur was going to catch the 2 p.m. train to Poona, leaving it at Kirkee to stay the night with Major England.
I am writing all this rather more than a week after we began our voyage .
MAY 24 Sunday, we are in the middle of the Red Sea where the heat is very trying and all the poor children are frantic with prickly heat. Personally, I am feeling much more comfortable than I did a few days ago for the heat and smells of the ship bowled me over from the very first and for the first four days I was sick and miserable, day and night. However, after various doses and no food but lemons and soda water for four days, I gradually managed to return to life and society and I am now very fit and quite enjoying the society of some extremely nice fellow passengers.
The children have been well and jolly all the time and are giving no trouble beyond the inevitable help and care that all children of their age require.
I have just been looking back to my diary during my outward voyage two years ago and I think we are almost exactly in the same lat. and long. as we were on May 24, 1901.
MAY 28 Three boiling days in the Red Sea were succeeded by a stiff breeze which delightful as it was in itself made the ship pitch and roll, quickly reducing me to a sickly sort of pulp. However, a good night's rest put me all right and it is cool enough to make sleeping in one's cabin quite pleasant. We reached Suez at 6 this morning and after being inspected by a plague doctor amused ourselves by making a few purchases from the bumboat men.
I am writing on the upper deck after lunch, the children peacefully sleeping in their berths while we glide almost silently along the canal with a glorious breeze to refresh us. The pilot says the temperature in the canal was 114 for three days last week so we are very fortunate.
MAY 30 We reached Port Said in the middle of the night and I was awakened by the many noises overhead attendant upon mooring. I

managed, however, to doze throughout the night and the children did not wake at all. We got up at 5 a.m. and for an hour or so were amused watching stores of fish, flesh, fowl and vegetables being taken on board. It was rather disappointing that no bumboat men came. The early hour and restrictions because of cholera causing their absence. About 7.30 we steamed away, passing Lesseps' huge statue with which I now felt quite familiar owing to my introduction two years ago. About midday we were off Alexandria, the lighthouse and various buildings being plainly visible through glasses. A glorious day with a perfectly calm blue sea and that freshness in the air which is so acceptable to those who have been East of Suez for any length of time. We are having today (30th) a rather sickly motion and it is a good deal warmer. Tomorrow we ought to see the coast of Crete.

JUNE 2 Yes, we saw Crete right enough on the morning of the 31st but oh! what a day we had, an awful swell and a choppy sea! I began to be ill in the middle of giving the children their bath but managed to go through with it. By the time I had dressed them, however, baby also succombed and as it was bitterly cold she and I at once took to our berths. Ruthie braved the weather and the motion until after lunch when she joined us and from that time until about 8 p.m. we were being sick, one against the other, and very miserable we all were. A very pleasant lady passenger kept well and paid us one or two friendly visits and the good old stewardess was also kindly attentive. All things however come to an end and the morning dawned at last warm and sunny and we all awoke none the worse for our previous day's adversity. The evening was exquisite with a bright moon and stars shining over a perfectly calm sky. About 8.30 nearly everyone came to the saloon where we passed the evening with music and singing and watching some clever card tricks.

We went to bed about 10.30 not noticing any change in the weather but it seems that the captain had gone on the bridge at 9 p.m. as the light of Cape Spartivento had not been seen. In the middle of the night we were nearly all awakened by the melancholy howl of the fog horn and from then until the early dawn we were cheered by this music. I could make out from my port hole that we were in a dense mist. It was not until midday, when we met the captain at lunch, that we heard

Bungalow at Poona . Rear Helen & Georgina
front. Baby (Rachel) Willie? Ruthie & Lena (donkey)

that we, with four or five other ships, had gone about half way through the Straits of Messina when the fog got so bad that no lights could be distinguished. As this is, even in day light, a difficult bit of navigation, the captain decided to turn about and put back outside the Straits where we found ourselves at 5.30 a.m. today, June 2nd.

Even at this time the fog was very dense and I was afraid that we should get no view either of the Italian coast nor of Sicily. However, by 8 o'clock the mist rose and we had a lovely view of both, also of Etna, snow capped and, in an hour or two, Strombolie in a state of rather active eruption.

Just after getting through the Straits of Messina we had a terrific gale from the land, so bitterly cold that everyone rushed below for the warmest clothes that could be found. But directly we got again into the open sea it became quite hot and has been by far the warmest day we have had since leaving Port Said.

JUNE 4 Arrived at Marseilles about 1 p.m. but were kept in quarantine for several hours and did not get into dock till about 5.30. It was awfully cold and rough, with a fearful swell all night and today, even riding at anchor in the bay, it was horrible and I was horribly ill again, and the children too. All the people leaving to cross the Continent were away by 6.30 and I must say that I much envied them for they would be in London within 30 hours while we have to stay six days here and then have a further voyage of eight days.

However, those of us who remain all get on well together and we mean to pass our time as pleasantly as possible.

JUNE 5 Such a quiet peaceful night I awake feeling nearly all right, only looking rather like an owl.

In the afternoon nine of us, including four children, took a tram and went through some very good zoological gardens (free) and afterwards had tea at a lovely restaurant where we all did justice to the excellent chocolate, coffee and confectionery. After dinner I was persuaded, rather against my inclination, to go with Mr and Mrs Simcox and several others to a Music Hall. The entertainment was very fair and the spectators caused me much amusement. After the entertainment was over we sat in a boulevard cafe (on the pavement!) some of the party partaking of refreshment. We did not get back to the ship until past midnight.

JUNE 7 Sunday. A terrible collision took place just outside the harbour about mid-day. Two French ships, belonging to the same company, one just starting for Corsica with many passengers and the other just returning. They were rounding a small island at 14 knots and the homeward boat caught the other amidships sinking her in a very short time. A very great number of people have been drowned though the exact number is not known. Although so near, we heard nothing of the catastrophe until several hours afterwards.

We had a very pleasant outing after tea today. Three of us ladies and four children took trams and went out to a part called "La Corniche". Up and down hill we rushed, through boulevards crowded with gaily dressed merry throngs and along the coast past sheltered nooks with the "Bains de Mer" establishments looking very snug and inviting. It was, however, too late in the day to see any bathing parties. Baby's 3rd birthday.

JUNE 8 I went out directly after breakfast with a lady passenger who speaks French fluently and did some shopping. The shops are really lovely and I longed for wealth in order to buy dainties for friends at home; as it was I laid out as much as I could afford for the children.

Rain fell about 5 p.m. and continued throughout the evening thus preventing us going to a cafe as we had arranged to do.

JUNE 9 A heavy thunderstorm and a regular monsoon rain greeted us this morning. It is disappointing not to be able to get out for we have all been thoroughly enjoying land life in lovely weather ever since the morning after our arrival. The worst of it is, however, that these dock labourers won't work in the wet and are far too independent to obey any orders against their inclination; consequently, instead of taking in new cargo, as we ought to be doing, the day is just being wasted and instead of getting away tomorrow afternoon we shall be delayed still longer.

JUNE 13 Saturday. Just a month today since we left Bombay. We are now coasting Spain having left Marseilles at mid-day on the 11th. We are going slowly as the Captain does not want to reach Gibralter until day break tomorrow. No business can be done there between sunset and sunrise and he prefers to be spending the time at sea instead of anchoring for the night in the Straits. We plunged right into bitter cold as soon as we left Marseilles and this, added to considerable motion and a nasty trembling sensation owing to the screw being higher on account of carrying a lighter cargo, made me horribly ill again yesterday. Today it is smooth and much warmer though a fresh breeze makes one glad to wear warmest clothes.

JUNE 17 We reached Gibralter on Sunday morning, the 14th, about 6 a.m. A message came round to the cabins saying breakfast would be ready at 7.30 for any who wished to go ashore. I was one who got ready and by 8.30 nine of us went off in a steam launch, reaching the quay in about seven minutes. We walked down the principal street (a very narrow one) where, being Sunday, most of the shops were shut. Following our noses we found ourselves in some rather good public gardens where Eastern and Western plants were hob nobbing in a rather unusual way. Orange trees bearing ripe fruit and castor oil plants with berries rubbing shoulders with hollyhocks, stocks and lobelia. Geraniums were growing in huge bushes. A winding walk around took us near a part of the fort where notice boards warned us that "trespassers will be prosecuted". So there was nothing for it but to stick to the dusty white road which, with a very bright sun, caused an unpleasant glare. I was particularly taken with the funny old Spanish market women, some of them of huge proportions, seated on stout donkeys, with big paniers of fruit and vegetables on either side.

1904 to 1905

S.S. ASIA

JAN 15 1904 From Gibralter to Liverpool, sea sick, cold and anxiously excited, reached Liverpool on June 20th.

Pleasant stay with the Bloods for five days. Five weeks in lodgings (City Walls) at Chester renewing many old friendships and thoroughly enjoying time with mother, Olive and Helen and the little ones. Seven weeks at Cantalupe House, Dersingham (Norfolk). Cold, wet weather generally. Numbers increased by Georgie and Ilex, later by Uncle J. Baker. Milly French and three girls stayed near for a fortnight greatly adding to my pleasure. One month in London (14 Carlton Vale) all bustle and hard work.

Oct 20 Embarked at Liverpool on S.S. Olympia - Anchor Line, with babies.

NOV 15 Arrived Bombay. Two days in Bombay with Mr Keatinge, ten days Poona Hotel, Poona. Three days camp at Akawadi. Arrived at Singhur on Nov. 25th. Mr Rowlandson stayed from Dec. 24th for ten days.

JAN 7 Went down hill for one night camp at Akawadi then two nights at Karakwasla where Colonel Channer paid us a visit. Returned to Singhur on the 10th.

JAN 12 Started camping again and reached Arvi leaving on the 14th at 7.30 a.m. reaching Kapar Wahul at 2 p.m. Found Engineers' tent ready pitched for us; a very bare, uninteresting place and very glad of the big luxurious canvas house. We stayed here longer than intended because we found Mr Hanckel (Engineer) and his wife were staying at Bhat Ghur and as we wanted to make a little return for his kindness in lending the tent we asked them to spend a day with us. Left early on the 18th and did an extra long march to make up for lost time. Halted at Shirwal for breakfast about mid-day and had a hot afternoon going to Khandala by a very bare road, nearly all the other roads had been nice and shady. Arrived at Khandala at about 4 p.m. only just in time to get tents pitched before dark.

JAN 19 Arrived at Surrel after rather an uninteresting march up and down a Ghat road.

JAN 20 Arrived at Wai about 11 a.m. and having brought breakfast in my waggon we had it at once; the other carts soon arriving we had tents up and all camp ready by 1 p.m. Have made arrangements to go up to Mahabaleshwar tomorrow and stay the night.

JAN 21 Started with children at 7.30 in a shabby old carriage drawn by four mules and galloped straight away for about five miles. The road then became less steep and the leaders were taken off at the end of the sixth mile. Our wheelers were changed at a roadside stable for two lean horses one of which, on being harnessed, jibbed and "played the ass" for some minutes and I felt sure we should be turned over. However, the cunning old beast suddenly decided to go and, giving a plunge forward, we were soon galloping along to Panchgani. It is a very pretty little place, well wooded with fine trees and containing a post and telegraph office, bazaar and twenty or so nice looking bungalows. Unfortunately plague has made its way here the last two years and every shop was vacated while a few of the owners had migrated to the fields and exposed their wares for sale by the side of the road. Many streams were running down the hill sides in this neighbourhood and watercresses grew thickly by the side of the road. We were refreshed by a nice homey sight here too by bracken growing in profusion. From this place to Mahabaleshwar, nine miles ahead, the road only rises very gradually, the country around very hilly and exquisitely wooded is most picturesque and the fresh mountain air almost cold at 10.30 a.m. The soil is here a rich red colour, the rocks being the same tint and although the warm tint blends beautifully with trees and sky, making the general view more beautiful, the dust caused by constant traffic on the road is most unpleasant and ruinous to clothing. The lovely ferns and huge bushes of wild roses fringing the roadside are all smothered with it too.

Nearing Mahabaleshwar one finds an immense deal of cultivation, the hills cultivated here and there, where water is plentiful, in terraces to the very tops, while for three or four miles on either side of the stream in the valley everything is given up to fruit and vegetables, strawberries, raspberries, potatoes, lettuces and other English vegetables growing to special advantage.

We reached Mahabaleshwar about 11 a.m. and going straight to the Ripon Hotel found it absolutely empty except for the proprietor and a very small staff of servants. Having chosen our rooms and given orders for food we set out at once to explore the place and found our way to

Ruth aged 4 Rachel aged 2

Government House. We rested in the grounds on seats specially placed for fine views and climbed to the flag staff which is probably on the highest part of the hill.

There was a dense mass of locusts passing over Mahabaleshwar making terrible havoc as they went of the young shoots from the trees. I can give but little idea of numbers which were "innumerable" but the noise of the fluttering of myriad wings was like the burr of some vast machine.

After wandering about until we were tired we returned to the hotel for tea to which, after being washed and brushed, the children did special justice, eating the whole of a good sized chicken between them.

After tea we had another stroll, going through the bazaar which appeared well stocked with all the ordinary European and native goods. Hot baths at the Ripon, succeeded by bread and milk, reduced the children to a healthful state of drowsiness and they were no sooner tucked into their beds than they were asleep. We also retired early and had a long night's rest.

JAN 22 After chota hazri and a leisurely toilet we took the children for a good walk over the golf links returning for breakfast at 10.30. After this I went to the only English shop to try and get some picture post cards with views of the place but failed in my object. Arthur, meanwhile, took the children for a more interesting stroll. After a cup of tea and a plantain, having got our bags packed earlier, we were ready for the return journey and got away a little after 2 p.m., reaching camp in 2 1/2 hours changing horses twice on the way as we had done going up.

JAN 23 Day in camp at Wai.

JAN 24 Camp half way to Khandala.

JAN 25 Day in camp at Khandala, My birthday.

JAN 26 Camp near Shirwal.

JAN 27 Camp at Kapar Wahul.

JAN 28 Day in camp. Mr and Mrs Hanckel came to breakfast.

JAN 29 Camp at Arvi, the same as on January 12th. Went out by moonlight with Arthur to try and shoot a wild pig; we saw a good many but could not get near enough for a shot.

JAN 30 Again went out and sat up for pig from 9.30 p.m. till 3 a.m., but without success. We got a hare which, however, was better than nothing. The natives made us a big bed of nice straw in which Arthur nearly buries me as the nights are rather cold and I get a sound sleep during the long waiting times.

JAN 31 Arthur went a third time for pig, without success. I intended to have gone but after dinner was so tired I went straight to bed.

FEB 1 Returned to Singhur.

FEB 3 Arthur went to Poona for Bombay.

FEB 12 Mrs Hanckel came.

FEB 13 Arthur returned to Singhur with three horses. He stayed only one day in Bombay, then stayed in Poona for two and afterwards went on to the camp at Arvi where he had better chances of trying the horses than at Singhur. He came up each alternate day to see us until he returned on Feb. 13th.

FEB 20 Mrs Hanckel, children and I walked down to Akarwadi and joining Arthur there spent the day in the valley.

FEB 22 Ruthie's birthday.

FEB 23 Geoffrey came.

FEB 26 Arthur and Geoffrey took the horses and went to camp at Arvi.

FEB 27 Plague of locusts. Five missionaries came to tea.

FEB 28 Another visitation of locusts but they all disappeared after flying round for about an hour. found small, deadly snake in my bathroom, butler killed it at once.

FEB 29 Arthur and Geoffrey returned from Arvi and on March 3rd Geoffrey left for Bombay.

MAR 12 Arthur and I went down for day in valley leaving children with Mrs Hanckel. Rode "Hazel Nut", put her over a wall or two and tried her across some ploughed fields.

MAR 16 Mr Hanckel came and on the 16th Mr and Mrs Hanckel left.

MAR 22 Went down with children, servants, horses, hounds, donkey, sheep and fowls, to Arvi camp. Very hot during day, beautiful in early mornings and fair at night. Arthur up nearly every night after pig which come in herds to destroy, or rather feed upon wheat crops. Shot several but only got two, these proved most excellent food.

MAR 31 Arthur and I rode up to Singhur starting at 6 a.m. Had breakfast there, wrote several letters and did various things in garden, etc. Returned to camp about mid-day. Late in the afternoon had thunder, lightning and some heavy rain which threatend to flood our tents but fortunately left off before soaking through. During the night a terrific wind got up and we had a lot more thunder and lightning. Arthur, who was sleeping under a tree, hurried his bed into my tent fearing more rain but we had only a few drops.

The trees in a neighbouring valley are absolutely red with locusts but we have so far only seen a few stragglers here. The storm has cooled the air considerably which is delightfully fresh and balmy if one can only find shelter from wicked old Sol's rays to enjoy it.

APR 1 Good Friday. Heavy rain about 4 p.m. It cleared in about an hour and we went off to shoot "for the pot" but got caught in a heavy storm, thunder, lightning and rain, and returned with only one pigeon, just enough for breakfast, however.

APR 7 Returned to Singhur and on the 9th Dr and Mrs Thompson came to the hill.

APR 21 Colonel Channer spent the day with us.

APR 23 Major England came about 6 p.m.

APR 24 Major England left after tea.

APR 30 Mr Armstrong came.

MAY 2 Mr Armstrong left. Arthur rode down with him to Akawadi, starting soon after 6 a.m.

MAY 9 Called at 2 a.m. Arthur left soon after 3 a.m. with horses and hounds. There had been thunder and signs of coming rain for several days and this afternoon, about 3.30, a tremendous storm of rain and hail fell, hail stones an inch across, perfectly smooth and round, fell in hundreds, to the children's huge delight. Poor Lena, the pet donkey, the only animal left with us, after enduring patiently for some time outside, came into the house for shelter!

MAY 11 Georgie and Helen arrived at 7.15 p.m.

MAY 21 Arthur, Mr Armstrong and Arthur T. rode up arriving about 6 p.m. and we all walked down the riding path to meet them.

MAY 23 Two Arthurs and Mr Armstrong left at 7 a.m. and we walked as far as the cave with them.

JUNE 15 All went to Poona and stayed for a few days in Colonel Bull's house as our cottage was not ready.

JULY 7 Hunting proper began, meet at Government House. Poona season full of gaieties, as ever, but failure of rains caused much sickness and a great many deaths from cholera, dysentry and enteric.

SEPT. to NOV Sport very poor until September when a few heavy showers put the country into better hunting condition - a depressing season in all ways. Hunting conditions much improved towards the end of the season but many hounds died from some most obstinate internal disease. Baby had opthalmia and later an obstinate attack of fever. Georgie got enteric and after being in bed six days at home was sent to the Sassoon Hospital where she stayed five weeks until convalescent.

DEC 3 We all went to Bandra, Georgie joining us at the station from the hospital.

DEC 4 Went to the beach before breakfast and were much interested watching the fisher people bring in an immense quantity of fish.

DEC 5 Rode before breakfast with Arthur. We went to the kennels at Santa Cruz, about 1 1/2 miles from here, then did a long round of explorations.

DEC 6 Beach before breakfast with the children and afterwards at about 1.30 went to Bombay with Arthur for a little shopping.

DEC 8 My first day with Bombay Hounds, slow hunting and not much sport, but a pleasant outing. Had coffee and fruit afterwards with several other hunting folk at the Jackal Club, Santa Cruz.

DEC 10 All started at 7 a.m. to spend the day on an island near. Being only accessible at low tide we had to choose our time. Arthur rode and Ruthie also on Lena. Helen, baby and I walked while Georgie went in a bullock cart, with rugs, cushions and food for the day. We took two native "boys". We boiled a kettle for breakfast under the shade of cocoanuts which grow densely all over the small island and quite down to the beach which has a magnificent stretch of sand at low water. At high water, about 2 p.m., in improvised bathing dress, we had a family bathe, all of us except Georgie who thought it wiser to "paddle" only. Ruthie made excellent attempts at swimming with her father, and baby was absolutely happy rolling over in the warm sea water. Helen and the little ones bathed in "topees" giving them a comical effect. Arthur and I, thinking our skulls sufficiently mature to withstand the sun, dispensed with ours and took no harm.

A polite old native on the island supplied us with fresh water from his well and also sent his son up a high tree to get us green cocoa nuts. They contained each about a pint of "milk", the nutty part being undeveloped and forming only an inner coating of rather tasteless, creamy, slimy white stuff. The milk which is as clear as spring water was absolutely cold and had a very slight flavour of cocoanut with a suspicion of acid which made it extremely refreshing and drunk from the nut itself cut into a sort of cup by the natives. We got home about 7.15 p.m. after a thoroughly enjoyable day.

DEC 11 Arthur had a fall out hunting and came back very stiff and sore. A hot bath improved him, however, and he and I went by previous invitation to tea at Santa Cruz with Mr "Xit" Remington, a former M.F.H. and a man well known in Bombay sporting circles.

DEC 13 Arthur still very stiff but nevertheless anxious for me to ride with him to find the lake from which the Bombay water supply is obtained. We started at 7.30 a.m. and reached the lake three hours later finding our watches exactly corresponded with the sundial there pointing to 10.30. The scenery here was very much like Windermere, an enormous lake with well wooded hills, undulating on three sides, the fourth being a big "bund" with a drop of many thousand feet to the stream and valley below. We got home, hot, rather tired (also a little bit raw!) and very hungry, at 1.30 p.m.

DEC 15 Second day with the Bombay Hounds. We had a splendid run and my little mare "Promotion Nut" carried me very cleverly. Arthur contented himself with pottering around as his shoulders and ribs were still painful.

DEC 17 Went to the beach before breakfast, the two little ones bathed. In the afternoon I took them by train to West Camballa Hill, Bombay, to a children's party given by Mrs Symington, a lady I had met in Poona three years ago. We did not get back till past 8 p.m.

DEC 18 Gave the children a sea bath before breakfast.

DEC 22 Jolly morning with Bombay Hounds. Colonel Bull returned with us after hunting to spend a few days. Ate oysters at dinner and was decidedly the worse for them next day.

DEC 23 Colonel Bull and Arthur went to Behar Lake for shooting but had no sport. They dined with Mr and Mrs Pike but I was unable to go

Colonel Arthur W. Sheringham

on account of "oyster riots". I spent most of the day in bed. Colonel Channer and Gertie arrived about 9 p.m. having missed the earlier train by which they intended to come.

DEC 24 Awoke feeling all right. Colonel Bull went to Bombay early. The rest of us, Arthur and I, Colonel Channer, Gertie, Georgie and Helen, went at 2 p.m. by train for an afternoon at the Exhibition. We returned in time for 8.30 dinner having been much interested in what we saw, though it was not nearly all. Mr and Mrs Pike dined with us.

DEC 25 Christmas Day. Many letters, cards and presents for the children. Spent a long day on Cocoanut Island. Arthur and I had a good swim taking the little ones into the sea with us where they enjoyed a good splash. Mr Burney dined with us.

DEC 26 Day with hounds. Good run. Colonel Bull left us after breakfast. Children went to a Christmas Tree Party at Mrs Pike's.

DEC 29 Jolly day with hounds. Ruth came on Lena and kept up wonderfully well. The M.F.H., Mr Lord, gave her the brush of the first kill and some gentleman asked to be allowed to take her photograph after the hunting, which he did and has promised to send me a copy.

1905 to 1906

S.S. ASIA

JAN 1. 1905 New Year's Day! Early morning took the children to the beach and gave them a swim. At 11.15 all went to church and enjoyed a nice, quiet, service in a pretty little building, St. Steven's Bandra Hill.

JAN 3 Picnic at Behar Lake. Arthur, Colonel Channer and Mr Pike rode, while Mrs Pike, Gertie Channer, Georgie, Helen, the chicks, "Jackie" and I went by train to Andheri and thence by tonga to Behar. The drive was terribly jolting and lasted for about an hour but, being sometimes through pretty scenery, we made the best of it. Mrs Pike and I took several photographs and the men got some good snipe shooting before breakfast. We all made a huge meal about 11 a.m., Mrs Pike supplying all the dainties including a spiced "Hump" of beef from Calcutta and I the more solid, but necessary, fare. About 1 p.m. we moved on by tonga to Powai Lake having arranged to meet the men folk there for tea. We started homeward about 5 p.m. and after tonga and train return journeys reached home about 7.30 after a very pleasant day.

JAN 4 After breakfast I went to Bombay with Arthur and Colonel Channer to do a little shopping. Afterwards I went to the Secretariat and had tea and a chat with Mrs Keatinge.

JAN 5 Capital morning with hounds. Arthur, Colonel Channer, Ruth and I started at 5 a.m. in pitchy darkness, a syce with "batti" to guide us. Colonel Bull, who was hunting and Captain Jennings, the man who took Ruth's photograph last week, returning with us for breakfast. We were a lively party of ten, all with excellent appetites. Colonel Channer left in the evening.

JAN 6 Gertie Channer left in the afternoon.

JAN 7 Arthur went to Bombay and I had a pleasant drive with Mrs Batty after tea.

JAN 8 Got up at 5 a.m. Georgie, Helen and I walked with Arthur as he rode by lamplight to Santa Cruz. After seeing hounds start we went on to Colonel Channer's camp, found Gertie (Channer) asleep. Stayed for a cup of tea. Helen and I returned, walking, at 8 a.m. leaving Georgie for a few days visit.

JAN 9 When chota hazri was brought the boy gravely informed us two of the syces had gone away in the night. Later I found the dhobi (washerman) had also decamped. Native servants are positive darlings!!

JAN 16 Arthur T. came for a short visit having been sent from Secunderbad to Bombay with a draft.

JAN 19 Nice day with hounds.

JAN 20 Arthur T. left.

JAN 21 Went with Arthur and Mrs Pike to Bombay Races. Had tea with Mrs Pike and met several Poona folk.

Dec 23 Started at 6.30 to go by train to Borivli, where Colonel Channer was camping. Mrs Pike with a friend and Jackie, Georgie, Helen, the little ones, Nellie Anderson and I.

On reaching Borivli, where Gertie met us, we started walking with three bullock carts following to pick us up when tired, to see some very old Buddhist caves. The road of about 3 1/2 miles was rather rough and very dusty, but very pretty; the trees, palms and bamboos meeting over head all the way. We occasionally got into the carts but, on the whole, the elders of the party preferred walking to being badly jolted. On reaching the foot of the hill we all halted and we all ate huge chunks of cake which I had provided. We left the little ones here to play and the servants to prepare breakfast. We then walked up a steepish hill path for another mile or so but as it was in dense shade we did not mind the walk at all.

It is difficult to describe the caves, of which we saw about a dozen. There are 104 in all and are supposed to be at the very least 2000 years old. Some are merely plain chambers with doorways and seats, something like those at Singhur, and apparently for human dwellings. Others are much ornamented with carvings, hundreds of representations of Buddha in various positions, from tiny things half a foot high, to life size and over while in front of the principal or "Cathedral" Cave, as it is now called , there are two colossal standing figures 22 feet high. There are many inscriptions on the walls, which I longed to be able to decipher but as they are in dead languages, Colonel Channer told us, they could only be deciphered by special experts employed by the Archaeological Society. Mrs Moir and Mrs Pike tried to photograph but the available spaces were so small and the light so shifting that they are afraid they will not be successful.

After spending a considerable time in the caves we walked down the hill and by this time, nearly mid day, we were all ravenous and did justice to a good breakfast provided by Gertie Channer. We lazed for several hours then had tea, after which we returned to Borivli as we came, intending to catch a train at 5.40 p.m. but, on reaching the station, were disconcerted at hearing this train ran on Saturdays only (it was then Monday!) so there was nothing for it but return to Colonel Channer's camp for two hours when we did get a train which brought us home very late for dinner. Arthur and Mr Pike were just beginning to get uneasy when we turned up.

JAN 31 Rode early with Arthur to Colonel Channer's camp. Gertie has been laid up for five days and has a nurse from Bombay. She got internal inflammation after a chill and was very ill for a time.

Mary, Miss Hogg and Georgie went to Bombay after an early breakfast and from thence by boat, to the caves of elephants. Helen and I very busy all day packing. Helen and the two little ones went to a tea party with next door neighbours.

FEB I am writing up my diary on February 4th and quite forgot I had said nothing of Mary Beck's visit. We learned on Sunday morning, 29th, that she would reach Bombay that afternoon so Arthur went to meet the "Malta" which arrived about 6.30 p.m. The party joined us at Bandara about 9 p.m. and were glad to have dinner at once. Mary was looking remarkably well and in brightest spirits. Had a long chat after dinner and did not go to bed till past midnight. On January 30th I forgot to say that I took Ruth to lunch with Lady Jenkins. Much amused with "Woomaru", the monkey, also heaps of dogs and many parrots. Afterwards went on to a children's fancy dress party. Ruth went in her khaki riding suit, with a black turban as the "Rajah of Bong". Lady Jenkins tied round her a string of amber beads, at least an inch and a half across, which much added to her appearance. She sent one of her servants to the party with me on purpose to bring them back as they are very valuable. Mary and Miss Hogg went to Bombay to make various arrangements.

FEB 1 Mary and Miss Hogg went with Georgie, Helen and Ruth to the same place where we had our picnic on Christmas Day. I spent my day at packing, letter writing and accounts. After tea Arthur took Mary for a ride.

FEB 2 Arthur and I had our last day with the Bombay Hounds. A ripping good run and kill. Afterwards another good run but lost the jack in the hills. Returning home we came across several men who had been hunting and were shocked to hear that Mr Xit Remington (a well known sportsman, called the Father of the Bombay Hounds, having been the first Master of them about 30 years ago) had just then, in the midst of chatting with his friends, fallen dead from his horse. It was known he had a very weak heart and had been for some time cautioned by doctors to avoid violent exertions. This sad event caused quite a gloom as Mr Remington was a most popular, kind hearted man, the attributes, I think, of most keen sportsmen. H.E.Lord Northcote was out hunting for the first time this Bombay season, he had a long chat with me, enquiring for Ruth and asking many questions as to what we had been doing since he last saw us.He invited us to go out and stay the night at Government House, Malabar Hill, for a ball on February 3rd but I asked if we might be excused on account of having made all arrangements for going into camp that day.

After breakfast Mary and Miss Hogg went off to Bombay preparatory to making their Indian tour. We said only "au revoir" as we hope to see them at Singhur as they have promised to come there after sight seeing just before they leave the country. Spent the day packing and making final "bandobast" (arrangements or settlements).

FEB 3 Started Georgie, Helen, the little ones, butler, cook and one syce, off by train to Thana (where the butler had already gone the day before to fix our camp) and after taking a final look round Arthur and I riding with a syce came with two bullock carts, Shiwa and the dog boy. We stayed, slowly, with the carts for the first four miles as the road for this distance was a rough country one, over paddy fields and many obstacles. Having seen them safely over this piece we rode on another twelve miles to Thana. We arrived in camp about 2 p.m. and were very glad to find breakfast ready for us immediately. The train wallahs had arrived about two hours earlier and had refreshed themselves. Had a quiet afternoon under the trees. Dinner and bed in good time;. mosquitoes rather bad at night as I had only taken care to put up curtains for the little ones.

FEB 4 After breakfast, Arthur having got news that there was snipe and quail shooting to be had about four miles distant, he and I, with

Georgina reading to Ruth (standing) Baby on her lap at the bungalow Singhur

Ruth, started in a "dummy" with a pair of ponies. Arthur wanted me to come but as I was not inclined for walking I brought Ruth as my companion and to get her out of mischief as, without her, baby will get her proper afternoon's rest. I may add that a "dummy" is a low, covered conveyance on two wheels, not unlike a London baker's cart.

I am writing this under a tree at Kolsett, quite near the huge Thana breek from which a cool breeze is blowing, with Arthur shooting quail all around. Presently we shall refresh ourselves with cake, plantains and beer, for we made our arrangements too hurriedly to bring all the etceteras for making tea. Arthur got five couple of quail and then we went back to camp where I was glad to have a cup of tea. Dinner and bed under mosquito curtains for I had suffered considerable damage from their attentions the previous night.

FEB 5 Called at 5 a.m. and after chota hazri and packing we five females started with one bullock cart and Lena an interesting road at first but improving as we went. Helen and I walked nine miles of the ten to the next camp. Georgie and the little ones preferring to make more use of the bullock cart than we did. There was a breeze the whole way and we were not at all tired. We found a police "chowki", a small bungalow for the care of engineers' tools here (Daisa) and as we decided to move on again early next morning we had only one tent pitched for ourselves and put the girls and babies into the house to sleep.

FEB 6 Called at 5 a.m. and tried to choke down a lump of dry bread with a cup of tea, we had run out of butter, our last supply having come from Bandra.

About 7.30 Helen and I started walking with the children, Georgie waiting to ride with her father. Lena was very troublesome and finding she could not get rid of Ruthie by kicking proceeded to lie down with her, repeating this trick on four different occasions.

After walking 4 1/2 miles we waited for the cart and put baby and Ruthie into it, tying Lena at the back. Helen and I then walked on and did the whole march to Panvel, eleven miles, on foot. Arthur and Georgie were very late in joining us, Arthur having stayed to shoot on the way. He got two green pigeon, two wild duck and one quail, so we have plenty of flesh for the day's pot. In the afternoon he wandered from camp with his gun and brought in three blue rocks.

Our camp here is on a little mound covered with trees, so thickly that we can only pitch the tents here and there where there is enough available space. We overlook on one side a huge water tank (oblong) with steps and terraces running the whole length of the four sides. We have our meals under the trees above when sunny and on the terrace below for chota hazri and dinner. We are quite entertained by the various types of people who come for water or to wash their clothes.

FEB 7 Arthur got up early, as usual, and went off to explore and shoot, if possible. He has just sent back, by a syce (9.30 a.m.) three snipe and a note saying he has come across some lovely lakes with any amount of duck, snipe, golden plover and quail, and that I am to try and make arrangements to have a boat tomorrow as the duck are impossible to get at without one. Helen has had a long rest after her exertions of yesterday and is only just waking a little before 10 a.m. Meanwhile, Georgie and I, with the little ones, have had a good walk through a big bazaar and on to a rough pier from which boats take rice straw, grass, etc., by the creak to Bombay.

The people here seem particularly friendly and polite and evince much interest in us and our doings. We, in turn, are much interested in them and their industries and we spend lots of time watching them turning hubs for cart wheels at a rough lathe, dividing cocoanuts from their huge husks, and also saw copper, brass and silver workers. I did a little bargaining at the latter place and bought an oddly shaped silver cow as a memento. I took a photograph of a street scene but I am rather afraid I moved the camera.

Arthur spent the day out by himself, shooting and looking for "Bountiful" who strayed from him whilst on the way from Daisar and who has, so far, not been found.

After breakfast, which we had unusually late, I took a photograph of dhobi folk at the tank and then tried a water colour sketch of the same tank with our camp overlooking it.

FEB 8 We all went out shooting with Arthur as soon as we were dressed, to a lake about 3/4 of a mile away. He waded above his knees and got eight snipe. We came back for breakfast after which Helen, Ruth and I went with him again to another lake where he had arranged to have a boat as although there were plenty of ducks here they calmly sat in the middle of the lake and refused to budge from stone throwing. By dint of rowing about for a considerable time he managed to get three. We, three, meanwhile, sat in the shade and I sketched the lake and surroundings. We afterwards walked to the big lake where we had been in the early morning and had the boat taken there on a bullock cart. But the ducks here, in great numbers, were too wild to get at so, after about an hour, we returned having spent a most enjoyable day and being provided with enough food for tomorrow. Our next destination is Vuandal and we learn there are no supplies to be had there.

FEB 9 Arthur and I rode, the others started walking. We found Georgie and baby sitting up in a tree about 4 1/2 miles on the road. I forgot to say, Ruth came on her donkey, Lena, with Shiwa and the bullock cart and near the sixth milestone we came across Helen stumping along, in such a determined way, that I offered her my mare to ride and I walked for a couple of miles.

Here we halted for a little, giving the horses grass and water. We found the village of Chauk, about twelve miles distant from Panvell and were rather disappointed to find our destination, Vuandal, was two miles further.

Arthur and I, with a syce, reached the camping place three quarters of an hour before the cart which Helen had joined after our rest above mentioned. It was nearly 1 p.m. and to save time, for we were wanting breakfast, I proceeded to collect fuel for a fire and directly the others came we dumped a chatty of water on to boil at once.

We feasted greedily on snipe, onions, bread and jam leaving....

I don't know what I was going to say for just as I had written so far there was a horrible thud and baby fell from a tree which she and Ruth were climbing. Fortunately she had on her topee, which broke the fall, but she has a slight cut and a nasty bruise on the back of her head. She turned rather white and was glad to lie down but I hope she is not really hurt.

Following this Ruth has just been discovered drinking unboiled water, the latter having come from a way side well of unsavoury appearance but being the only available water for this camp.

It has just occurred to me what I was going to say. Leaving ... nothing but bread, bones and beaks of snipe, with the thinnest possible potato parings for a hundred hungry crows who pestered us with their cawing pertinacity.

The carts, with tents, etc., only arrived about 4 p.m. so it will be almost dark before tents are pitched and everything ready for the night.

FEB 10 Helen and I started walking and after going 7 1/2 miles we found a shady place near a well and rested ourselves a long time before Shiwa and the little ones arrived with the first bullock cart. When they did come it was past 12 o'clock and they said Arthur had stayed behind to shoot so I did not know when to expect him. I decided, therefore, to boil a kettle there and have breakfast, which was just ready when Arthur and Georgie turned up. Although they had seen a good many duck and an enterprising native had floated out on a log to make them rise from the lake, Arthur couldn't get a shot. After breakfast we went a mile further and came to Campooli, a biggish village at the foot of the Ghat below Khandala. We decided to stay here a night instead of going on to Khandala as the Ghat road to that place, though only six miles long, is so steep that special arrangements have to be made for buffaloes instead of bullocks to drag the carts and we thought the servants would be glad not to have to go on any further.

The Patel of the village was summoned to supply grain and grass for the horses, also fowl, eggs and milk for ourselves. He then shewed us a good place for camping near a very picturesque Hindu temple. I have photographed this and also tried to sketch the place.

We are again on the edge of a huge tank surrounded by a massive stone wall with broad flights of steps at intervals round it. The ghats form a semicircle, or rather a perfect horse shoe nearly shutting us in so I expect the night will be considerably warmer than in our recent camps.

Arthur and Helen went out with the gun before tea but returned with one snipe only.

FEB 11 We all had a "Europe" morning and leaving the children and servants for a quiet day Arthur and I rode up to Khandala after chota hazri, starting only about 9 a.m. The Ghat road is very steep and very picturesque, massive rocks jutting out in pinnacles of gaunt grandeur from the lower hill sides, covered with dense jungle growth. As we got higher and higher the shrill whistle of a train seemed almost to desecrate nature and it gave me a mixed feeling of wonder and admiration at the daring and ingenuity of man, that he should be able to negotiate these mighty hills with his iron road over them and under them and, on it, run his locomotives bearing his precious human freight with apparently no more difficulty than a toy is moved at the will of a child.

It took us 1 1/2 hours, walking the horses at a fair pace, to reach Khandala and we were disappointed to find, after careful searching, that the only available camping ground was bare of trees and exposed to public view. There are plenty of trees but they are all in private grounds into which we could not intrude. We had already decided to bring up our party at night simply because the natives will not work their buffaloes up the hill in the heat of the day. So we called the Patel of the place and arranged with him to have supplies for the horses, with fire wood, eggs, etc., ready for us at 1 a.m. (after midnight). We called at the Post Office where we had given orders for our letters to await us and were disgusted to find that several had been delivered but as we had not called for them they had been sent back to Poona. The Post Master was, however, obliging and wired for them to be back by the following morning.

Having thus made all arrangements we went to the primitive, but well managed, little Khandala Hotel and did justice to an excellent breakfast, after which we dawdled about and read the papers before again riding down the hill. We got back to camp about 3 p.m. and after changing some of my riding kit for cooler attire I spent my time finishing a sketch I had begun the day before.

Meanwhile tents were struck and all packing done so as to start about 10 o'clock for our second journey up the hill. The little ones were allowed to have a somewhat substantial supper from our dinner table and were afterwards dressed warmly for their night journey. I got riding clothes again and by 10.30 we started, the little ones having been carefully "put to bed" in a cart by their father soon after dinner. Baby was already sound asleep when the jolty journey began.For a short distance until we arrived at the Ghat road the carts were drawn by bullocks but at this point they were unyoked and the huge, unwieldly and uninviting brutes of buffaloes were put in their places. Arthur and I, with the two girls, walked for a little distance and then he and I mounted and slowly, slowly, followed the lazy buffaloes. When we had gone a short distance Arthur found the bullocks, which were again to relieve the buffaloes at the top of the hill, were not following. So the syce had to be sent back to drive them forward and we waited until they caught us up.

I can hardly describe the pace that those awful buffaloes travelled. Arthur and I waited about every twenty yards, for at least a quarter of an hour. (This I have discovered would take 22 hours to do a mile, so you can imagine we went a bit faster than that.)

No sooner did we walk our horses quite slowly on than we came up with them. Once Arthur thought we would go forward and urge them on, but the sight of his horse was apparently so alarming to them that two pairs suddenly bolted round and got quite off the road with their heads alarmingly near the edge of the khed (ravine). The drivers have absolutely no control over them if they choose to take the law into their own hands, so to speak, for they only have a rope round their horns. They are fastened into the carts with two wooden pegs which fit closely on either side of the neck onto which is fastened a sort of string net which passes under the buffalo's neck and is looped either side over the pegs.

Finding it was useless to try and increase the speed of travelling we therefore resigned ourselves to the inevitable and as the little ones were both now fast asleep and the girls driving in their wagon also, we made our halts rather longer and several times snatched a short sleep as we sat in our saddles. This went on, it seemed, for an eternity and when, after one or two more exhibitions of ill temper on the part of the buffaloes, we at last reached our destination, we found it was 3.30 a.m., the journey having taken exactly five solid hours!!

It was decidedly cold now and we at once set to work, or rather set the servants to work, to boil a kettle so as to have a "cup that cheers" etc. We left the children fast asleep, still in their cart and covered them warmly with blankets. Then Arthur collected the hay, which the

Patel had in readiness for the horses. He made a huge bed, spread it with blankets and tucked the girls and me snugly up in more blankets. We giggled at the novelty of the situation, three women (like Blue Beard's wives, I said) laid out at length on the ground in the middle of the night, with a chilly wind blowing, and the stars blinking and winking in wise superiority above us.

In spite of this regular bivouac we all managed to sleep comfortably for a couple of hours, or so, and at 6.30 a.m. were glad of another cup of tea and a munch of bread and butter.

We had some difficulty in persuading the children to wake and join our refreshments but when we had accomplished this we made up our minds to start with them and the donkey for our next camp, leaving Arthur with the carts until supplies were bought and letters delivered.

We took our time and though we felt rather disreputable, for we walked on as we had slept without the chance of a wash, we were all quite fresh and vigorous.

After walking about four miles, having waited to rest in the shade several times, Arthur overtook us with bulging pockets. He soon produced a big parcel of sandwiches, a bottle of soda water and a lot of English letters, all of which we enjoyed immensely.

After sitting for a time Arthur rode on taking baby on his horse and I got onto the mare for I was, all this time, in riding kit and my riding boots were chafing my heels.

We reached Karli about 11.30 a.m. and found a perfectly ideal camping ground, a slight eminence and sufficiently covered with huge trees to make dense shade over about two acres with yet enough room between to pitch tents without any difficulty. A well of excellent water within a few yards and the village and post office not more than five minutes walk distant.

We stretched ourselves on the ground, thickly strewn with leaves, and rested comfortably until the cart followed with breakfast which was soon made ready and quicker still devoured. We spent the rest of the day quietly enjoying the peaceful surroundings.

FEB 13 After a rather longer night's rest than usual we all started to see the caves, Arthur and baby riding, the rest of us walking, as it was only a mile across country to the foot of the hill. Helen and I got a good deal ahead of the others and tackled the rather steep ascent with firm wills; it was a bit of a grind though and Arthur dismounted when about half way up out of consideration for his horse. Lena came up all the way, baby taking an occasional ride when she got tired of walking.

The caves were well worth a visit: it would take too long to describe them in detail but they are far bigger, more ornamental and in a better state of preservation than those we lately saw at Kanheri. Though not so numerous they are dated B.C. 200 so are the same age as those at Kanheri and are also Buddhist. At Karli the pillars of the "Cathedral" cave are most elaborately carved, as are also the panels of the outer court which is shaped like that at Kanheri, but in place of the enormous statues of Buddha there are the heads of gigantic elephants. They probably had ivory tusks originally fitted into their stone heads as each figure has two holes as if for the fitting of tusks. Some of the outer pillars were demolished by Hindus about 300 years ago and they erected a temple to their own gods on this site. The latter is decorated with many bells of various shapes and sizes and forms, a quaint contrast in its somewhat tawdry style to the majestic stone forms standing grimly sentinel like around. There are several flights of stone stairs cut through the rocks leading to upper chambers and these were all formed alike, one huge room with small ones running round three sides of it, each with its own little door way and compartment, probably the homes of the Buddhist monks who dwelt here and conducted the religious services.

When we had spent an hour or so exploring and investigating, the others all went back for breakfast but I stayed for a considerable time to sketch and take photographs. I got back to camp about 1.30 hot, hungry and thirsty, having had only a cup of tea and slice of toast before rising, but well satisfied with my morning's employment.

FEB 14 Arthur and I rode and the others walked and drove in the bullock cart to our next camp, Wadgaon, where the native Magistrate received us most courteously. He spoke perfect English and made all arrangements for getting all necessary supplies.

In the evening Arthur wandered out with his gun, taking Ruth and Helen, but only got a quail.

FEB 15 The youngsters started off fairly early, with Lena and their bullock cart. Arthur and I rode and made a considerable detour to a spot where we knew there ought to be some shooting. We went to two big lakes where wild duck were literally swarming, but they took excellent care to keep well out of the reach of a gun. We reached Nigri rather late and found the children had selected a shady place, near a well, and had already breakfasted.

As soon as we arrived they, one and all, poured tales of woe into our ears and they really had had a nasty accident. It appears that the bullocks in their cart were new to their work and our syce, thinking to hurry their pace, was driving them instead of their own master. This, and perhaps an umbrella being held in the air by one of the girls, upset their nerves and they suddenly swerved off the road and completely upset the cart, turning out the four children and all the rest of the paraphernalia. Georgie got the worst of it with a bruised cheek, a swollen nose and slightly black eye, also a general feeling of bruises. Baby had a cut on her knee and Helen various small cuts and abrasions. Effervescent Ruth continued to babble with mirth, as usual, and apparently popped up from the debris unhurt whilst three umbrellas were hopelessly smashed.

However, things might have been so much worse that everyone was content to take them as they were and we spent the rest of the day in settling into our new camp.

Just as it was getting dark, Mr Armstrong drove up. Arthur had sent postcards to both him and Colonel Channer saying we should be within easy reach and asking them to come out and have a meal with us. Mr Armstrong stayed to dinner and a long chat afterwards, not leaving till about 10.30 p.m., having made us promise all to stay with him on our way to Poona. He arranged to drive out and fetch the children the following day and Arthur and I were to follow the next morning after.

FEB 16 Had a long day out with Arthur. Had bad luck with shooting and got only a quail and some other bird. I had special amusement in seeing the sacred fish fed by Brahmins. The fish (marseer) have grown to an enormous size, 12 or 14 feet long and being shouted to by a native man and woman rose to the surface and dashed in and out the water taking huge mouthfuls of ground nuts which had been thrown for them and were floating on the water. We got back to camp for tea

The Dummy, Poona.
Left to right Georgina, Arthur Junior Ruth, Helen, Rachel

and at about 5.30 Mr Armstrong drove for the children and took them off to his charming home at Dapuri.

FEB 17 Arthur and I, being alone in camp, did not hurry ourselves as the other two tents, etc., had all been packed up the night before. When we started for Dapuri, about 8 o'clock, Arthur told the syce to bring his gun as he intended to ride across country to Dapuri and thought he might see some peafowl in a spot where he had often noticed them when out hunting. Sure enough, when we reached the place, we saw two fine cock birds feeding in a wheat field. They, however, noticed us as quickly as we did them and quickly hid. Arthur had got off his horse and taken his gun at first sight of them, however, and had marked one into a nullah (ravine) from this he presently emerged and Arthur fired. But he was rather far away and the bird flew away. Again we marked him and sending the syce one way, we went the other. The wary bird kept his sharp eye on us too and did all he could to dodge and evade us, flying, running and hiding, in turn. We had a most exciting chase for, when he flew, we had to gallop to keep him in view. Then, when he settled, Arthur tried to stalk him and eventually, after quite an hour's hunt, he shot him in a stony glen where he tried in vain to find covert.

We then rode fast to Dapuri for it was already past the breakfast hour at which time we had promised to arrive. Mr Armstrong quite forgave our unpunctuality and wished he had been with us in our wild peacock chase - not a wild goose chase by any means.

FEB 17 Three very pleasant days at Dapuri. Mrs Armstrong was away from home but Miss Murphy made an excellent substitute and Mr Armstrong was kindness itself.

FEB 22 Ruthie's 7th birthday. Arthur and I went by evening train to Belgaum, a visit we had long promised ourselves. We took dinner with us and afterwards slept comfortably arriving at Belgaum soon after 9 a.m. on the 23rd. Arthur had met an old friend in his compartment, his other fellow passenger being an R.C. Lord Bishop, the latter, as well as the other Major, were glad to share our chota hazri.

FEB 23 Spent most of the day, as well as yesterday, driving round cantonments and city, to see all Arthur's old haunts when commanding the Cheshires in Belgaum. It is a very pretty, well wooded place, with very red roads like those at Mahableshwar and though I saw it in the driest season it had a greenish tint everywhere.

Everyone uses "dummies" here and they are most roomy and comfortable conveyances, just the things for large families with small means and we carried out a long thought of project and bought one before leaving.

We returned to Poona by slow train (24 hours) on purpose that our new toy might come by the same train and when we reached Poona, about mid-day on the 26th, Shiwa was sent off at once so that by the time the dummy was off the truck the bullocks were ready. We put ourselves and our luggage into it and drove up to the house, much to the children's surprise and delight for a letter I had written from Belgaum, telling them when to expect us, had never reached them.

MAR 2 Mary Brek arrived about 8 p.m. for a flying farewell visit on her way from Umballa to Bombay. Arthur and I met her with the dummy but we had bullocks and she did not get a good idea at all of this mode of locomotion. At her special request we had a tent pitched for her to sleep in and she said she had never enjoyed a night's rest more for, after a train journey of two days and nights, a stationary bed was a peaceful luxury.

MAR 3 Mary and Arthur rode before breakfast. Georgie and Gertie Channer, with whom Georgie is staying, turned up for breakfast. Mary and Helen went out in a tonga after tea as we couldn't get bullocks for the dummy. They returned in time for Mary to have a bath before dinner soon after which it was time to go to the station to catch the mail train to Bombay. Arthur and I, afterwards, quite enjoyed a moonlight walk (nearly two miles) back from the station and got home about a quarter of an hour before mid-night.

MAR 6 Family Vaccination!! barring Georgie who was not quite well. Arthur and I dined with Colonel Bull.

MAR 8 Ash Wednesday. Helen, the little ones and I went to church at 7.30 a.m.

MAR 9 Arthur and I rode over to Dapuri to say good bye to the Armstrongs. We stayed to breakfast and had such a hot ride home that I was obliged to rest, intending to pack later on. However a note came from Mrs Anderson asking me to go for a drive at 4.30, which I did, by

Arthur's persuasion, and thoroughly enjoyed it.

MAR 10 Packing from 7 a.m. till 7 p.m. Rather hot and tired in consequence.

MAR 11 Many things to arrange; servants rather slow and tiresome. Georgie went at 7.30 to the Staff Hospital and as soon as she returned she, Helen and baby, started in the dummy, with Ruth riding behind. They took breakfast and Arthur and I, riding by a short cut across country, over-took them at the 8th milestone where we stopped and had breakfast. We got into camp (Karakwasla, the same as January 8th, 1904) about 3 p.m.

I was very tired and headachy so I did nothing more than I was obliged but as the cook lost his way and didn't get to camp till nearly 7 p.m. and the butler did not come because his wife was ill, we were obliged to give a good deal of help so as to get the tents ready before dark. To save pitching a third tent and unpacking their beds we let the children sleep in the dummy, which they thought great fun.

MAR 12 Nice peaceful day in camp. An old Hindu, living near, with whom we had made friends when camping here 16 months ago, came and made salaams, also supplying us with milk, and bringing vegetables and fruit as a present.

MAR 13 Moved to Akawadi, only five miles distant and breakfasted under the huge trees where we have so often been. Afterwards pitched two tents here and had the dummy drawn close in for the children's sleeping apartment. Rather hot and dusty during the mid-day hours, but pleasant enough at other times.

MAR 14 Helen and I started at 7 a.m. to walk up Singhur, a considerable undertaking which we accomplished, without being over tired, in one and one quarter hours. We were greeted on arrival by our old servant, Gownida. (the pani wallah) and the first thing we did was to drink some of the delicious cold water which abounds here. Next we boiled some for tea which, having drunk, we rested half an hour and then set to work to unpack and arrange as many things as had been left here from last year and those which came up with us.

We had breakfast about 12 mid-day having brought food with us. We worked again, unpacking, and washing china and glass, and doing many other duties. Then we took a walk round our domain and after having tea for the fourth time since 6 a.m. walked down the hill reaching camp about 5 p.m. Enjoyed more tea! which Georgie had thoughtfully kept for us. She and the little ones came a little way up the hill to meet us as soon as they spied us coming down the winding, steep path.

MAR 15 Day in camp. Just after breakfast news was brought that the well known Singhur panther had killed a heifer a few hundred yards away. Arthur went to see and found the freshly killed beast, undoubtedly dispatched by the panther. Accordingly he gave orders for a hiding place to be made in a convenient tree near the kill and we sent a coolie off at once to Dapuri telling Mr Armstrong what had happened and asking him to come out that night with his rifle, as Arthur has only a gun.

We waited, hoping to see him before dark, but he didn't come and the panther quietly came at intervals and devoured his prey, at last taking the remains far away into the jungle. A letter came from Mr Armstrong the following morning saying that ours did not reach him until 6.30 p.m. so it was useless for him to start but he hopes we may hear of Mr Panther again and will let him know.

MAR 16 The girls, children and I walked up to Singhur by the riding path, bringing the mare and donkey to assist us on our way. We reached the cottage about 8.30 a.m. and, as usual, drank tea at once after which, with intervals for meals and rest, we did a hard day's work and got the house into comparative order.

MAR 17 Arthur joined us in time for breakfast having stayed at Akawadi one more day with the hope of getting some sport near the lake but, unfortunately, he found so many of the jungly places which in other years have held peafowl hare and deer cut down so that he saw absolutely nothing to shoot.

MAR 18 Everything now quite in order and we are revelling in the cool fresh air, with plenty of time to get through needlework to our hearts' content. The children are delighted to be in their old haunts, and to be bare footed, and it is a great relief to Arthur to be here without the anxiety of hounds.

MAR 23 Major England brought his sister in law, Miss Boyce Coombs for a day on the hill; they joined us at 4 o'clock for tea.

MAR 24 Mr Armstrong came. He and Arthur tried hard the next day to get the panther, but saw nothing of him.

MAR 26 Mr Armstrong and Arthur went to "Drunkaderri", got a hare and a pigeon.

MAR 27 Mr Armstrong and Helen fished all day, former got eight gold fish - Helen one fish and a bad blister on her neck! Next day Mr Armstrong left, very early.

APR 6 All spent the day on a neighbouring hill.

APR 8 Arthur went down to Akawadi after tea, sent up two splendid peafowl early next morning which he had shot.

APR 10 Major England spent the day with us, brought heaps of fruit, cakes and chocolate, presents for the old, and young, children, he said.

APR 13 Arthur came home to breakfast saying he had shot a deer but it had gone slowly down the khud and he had left a coolie and syce to find it. As they had not returned by mid-day he and I went out to look also. After a good deal of climbing up and sliding down hill we came upon the men who said they had looked <u>everywhere</u> without success. We hunted further, till 3 p.m., then returned very hot and thirsty, but Arthur was not at all satisfied with the thoroughness of the search for he was certain the deer was mortally wounded and could not have gone far.

APR 14 Arthur sent the coolie out again to look in a particular place and from thence, sure enough, he brought back the deer which had been a little eaten by birds of prey but, otherwise, none the worse for having been lost for twenty-four hours.

APR 18 Arthur and I with Shiwa, three syces and four horses, Copal with "Lena" and "Bountiful" started at 7.30 a.m. for Tamwari, which we heard was a place full of peafowl. We found it a much longer journey than we expected as we had to travel slowly on account of crossing a very rough pass in the mountains. We stopped at mid-day under some trees for breakfast and did not reach our destination until 4 p.m., very hot and thirsty. We had not a very nice camping ground but we managed to have a very pleasant little visit. There were swarms of peafowl on a neighbouring hill, but they were so near a village they seemed almost tame and, although the natives were keen to bring us

Mr. Armstrong. Anajee. Mr. Wiseman.
Capt. Hopwood.
M.F.H. N.F.A. Sargent Col. Bull
Col. Chaunes.
1905.

news of them, Arthur did not like to shoot more than one as we were in a native state and the Rajah, being a Brahmin, might have taken offence.

The peafowl Arthur shot, a young cock bird in full plumage, was the biggest I have ever seen and fed us throughout our six days camp; the breast alone must have had at least 4 lbs of solid meat on it.

APR 20 We moved our camp to Khed Shivapur, again a longish ride, but we found a shady camp by mid-day and soon shook down into our new quarters. After dinner, as soon as the moon was up, we went and squatted in a sugar field which we heard was much frequented by jungle pig at night, but we both fell asleep and returned after a couple of hours without a shot. Our eighth wedding day. (Md.20.4.97)

APR 21 Arthur's birthday. We spent this, and the two succeeding days, riding about and exploring fresh places. We saw heaps of deer, pig, peafowl, hares, quail, blue rocks, etc., but Arthur had a very idiotic coolie for a beater, who always did the wrong thing, so that very few shots could be obtained. On the 23rd we returned to Singhur in time for breakfast.

APR 24 Arthur tired and ailing.

APR 25 Arthur went to bed, feeling ill and feverish.

APR 26 Arthur no better. Sent to Colonel Bull for medicine.

APR 27 Arthur slightly better.

APR 28 Arthur worse, so I wrote and told Colonel Bull.

APR 29 About mid-day the girls and I were sitting in the dining room, all feeling rather miserable, when we heard a whistle and, to our joy, who should it be but Colonel Bull who, not being satisfied with my last report of Arthur, made a special journey out bringing medicine, ice and a bag full of medical appliances in case of need. He is a real brick - and such a friend.

After careful examination of Arthur he decided "liver" was the cause of fever and strongly recommended him to be brought to Poona. He had brought out a carriage, with a change of horses, and though Arthur did not at all wish for the move he allowed Colonel Bull to dictate arrangements. These were that he was to be carried down the hill next morning, early, then get into the carriage and come straight to his house.

APR 30 Called at 4.30. Finished packing and rode down behind Arthur's dhooly (litter). Found the carriage ready at the foot and drove straight to Staveley Road, Arthur stood the journey well.

MAY 4 Mr Armstrong drove me from Colonel Bull's house, starting a little before 6 a.m., to Akawadi where saddle horses met us and we rode up to Singhur. Arthur having been steadily improving since we got to Poona, I left him in Colonel Bull's care and returned to the children who were muddling along with very rough servants.

MAY 9 Arthur returned. The hounds which arrived in Bombay on the 5th were sold at once to a Rajah as they are not wanted for hunting in Poona until June and came out a month earlier than Arthur had ordered them. This gives Arthur three weeks' freedom from hound worries and Poona heat. Slight thunder and a very little rain during the afternoon.

MAY 14 Three Parsees came to tea. Very black clouds gathered about 5.30 p.m. Later heavy thunder, much lightning, raging wind and more rain for about half an hour. Also some rain during the night.

MAY 15 A rather more decided shower but still the rain is nothing to speak of.

MAY 25 Arthur and I started about 7 a.m., having sent the horses forward, to walk to Morderri. We shot a Buggla there and rode home by Kundenpoor and Anserwadi where we bought a lot of green mangoes for "mango fool" and got home at 10.30.

JUNE 1 to 6 Much packing and arranging. On the 6th said a final good bye to Singhur. Arthur and I rode to Poona, the children travelled in the dummy.

Throughout the month much calling and receiving of callers. Very busy in house, garden and kennels. Several times dined out and had many Sunday afternoon teas at home.

JUNE 26 The season, proper, began with the Governor's reception which old and young Arthur attended; Georgie, Helen and I had seats in the gallery as onlookers. Reception at Government House in the evening. The two Arthurs, Georgie and I went. Rain is much longed for, a very little having fallen. Poona is hot and stuffy and the little ones are not quite well.

JULY 6 Opening meet. Desperately heavy rain, the country round being an absolute bog. Ran a jack a few minutes but hunting conditions being quite impossible soon gave up and returned home drenched but feeling ten degrees cleaner and fresher for the process. Evening Arthur dined with Sir A. Hunter, Georgie and I with the Fultons.

JULY 7 Arthur, Georgie and I dined at Government House.

JULY 9 Arthur and I tea with the Sheppards to meet the Keatinges.

JULY 10 Young Arthur, Georgie and I went to the Ball at Government House.

JULY 13 Excellent day with hounds. Evening tea with Miss Moore.

JULY 18 Went to tea with little ones with Mrs Toogan Pronne.

JULY 19 Miss Murphy with Georgie and Sydney Armstrong, also three McIvers came to tea with us.

JULY 20 Excellent day with hounds. Two or three days very wet indeed.

JULY 24 Arthur and I dined with the Channers.

JULY 27 Hunt breakfast. Pouring wet. Provided for 50 and about half that number came.

JULY 30 Arthur out hunting and looking for lost hounds from 4.30 a.m. till 7 p.m.

AUG 3 Pleasant day's hunting. Kennel Meet. Very large field. Arthur T. left at night.

AUG 5 My first wedding day - 25 years ago!
Went with Arthur to the races. Saw one race then joined the girls and little ones and went to Kirkee to tea and chat with Mrs Jooks.

(There follows a number of entries of outings and teas with friends and neighbours)

AUG 22 Big, mixed, "At Home" at Council. Parsees, Hindus and Europeans - rather good music.

(Further dinners, at homes, and social gatherings are mentioned, almost on a daily basis throughout September)

SEPT 8 Friends to breakfast. Major Chesney arrived last night from England. We have put him up in a room at the Kennels which young Arthur used when he was here. Georgie and children went to Kirkee where Helen is staying with Dorothy Jukes. I went to tea with Mrs Paterson. This was a red letter day as I had my first motor drive. Colonel Paterson brought me home, taking me first a long way round,

Rachel, Mother, Ruthie. July 1902

which I thoroughly enjoyed.

SEPT 13 Hunted in the morning. Georgie and I went to the Western India Club Ball in the evening.

SEPT 14 Tea at home 4 p.m. - Tea at Mrs Lawrence's 4.30 p.m.! Tea at Mrs Hanckel's at 5.20 p.m.!!

SEPT 15 Captain Jennings came to breakfast - Dorothy and Eric Jooks came to tea - Colonel and Mrs Cahusac, Major Rawlins, Major MacKenzie, Mrs MacKenzie and Arthur T. came to dinner.

SEPT 16 Big Ladies Luncheon at the Club of Western India. Arthur, Georgie and I went as guests of Major Rawlins. Races afterwards.

SEPT 18 Argyll and Sutherland Highlanders Ball, to which I took Georgie. Children went to a birthday party at Mrs Lawrence's.

SEPT 19 Nine Pudumjies came to tea!

SEPT 20 Big Ladies Luncheon at Club of Western India, Arthur and I went as guest of the Governor's Staff. Races afterwards.

Later, Helen and I went to a prize-giving to native children at the Panch Howd's Mission. Helen went with the Cahusacs and Major Rawlins drove me. Afterwards he took me for a drive in a very pretty part near Parbati, where I have never been before.

SEPT 23 A French morning, in aid of Hunt funds.

SEPT 25 Horse Show. Arthur, Georgie and I dined at Magdale House. Met General Francis, cousin to Mrs Francis of .... and had much Norfolk news to discuss.

SEPT 26 Horse Show. Ruth and baby, with 14 other children, rode in the children's class for ponies and donkeys. Ruth rode Lena and baby a huge Egyptian donkey of Colonel Bull's. Every child had a prize.

SEPT 27 I took the little ones to their first circus which gave them unbounded pleasure.

SEPT 28 Excellent day's hunting, the last for me I expect as most of the hounds are sent away. Had friends to tea.

OCT 2 Finals of Open Polo Tournament.

OCT 5 Last day's hunting. Met at Harapsar. Terribly hot, but hounds ran well. Three days ago, when I was not out, they had almost the best run of the season - 50 minutes and a kill. Arthur's horse turned turtle over a blind wall and gave him a nasty fall but, beyond a bruising and considerable stiffness, he is not hurt.

Native Infantry Ball at the Gymkhana in the evening. Decorations extremely pretty and altogether a great success.

OCT 6 Point to Point Hunt races. I gave away cups to the winners.

OCT 7 Big Luncheon given by Committee Members of the Hunt in our honour. People were all very nice - 79 of them (exclusive of Arthur, Georgie and me). Colonel Bull made a very eulogistic speech and presented a silver salver to us on behalf of Members. Arthur's health was drunk, with musical honours, for which he returned thanks in a neat little speech.

OCT 9 Went for a ride with Arthur., at 6.45, sent hounds back and went on for a little shooting. Got a brace of grouse and a quail. Later Georgie, Helen and I went to a Purdah Party in the afternoon, given by Mrs Pudumjie. Afterwards we went on to the Gymkhana and Gertie Channer took Georgie home to dine and stay the night.

OCT 12 The last of the hounds went away. Arthur quite forlorn. Georgie went to a Moonlight Picnic <u>and got back at 1 a.m.!</u>

OCT 13 Rode early with Arthur.

OCT 14 Helen and Georgie went to Assault at Arms. I packed the first box for England!

OCT 16 Arthur rode with two syces, the girls, babies and I went in the dummy and spent a real lazy day near Pashan Lake. We hoped young Arthur would have come but at the last he couldn't get away. We enjoyed the idleness but it was too hot to be perfect and Arthur got no shooting.

OCT 20 Four hard days packing.

OCT 21 We intended to have left the cottage today and gone into tents pitched in the Kennel Compound, but for the last ten days there has been such heavy rain, daily, we were obliged to decide last night to keep the house until the middle of November and postpone the auction from October 26th to November 7th. Rather a relief to me as I can finish packing more leisurably. Georgie, Helen and the little ones went to tea with the Pudumjies this afternoon and Arthur went to the Races. I was glad to have a good rest when all these frivolous young people had gone and before they returned. Arthur T. came for a chat and Arthur dined at the Club with Colonel Bull.

OCT 22 Young Arthur dined with us and brought a hare which he had shot.

OCT 23 The girls and I went with the Pudumjies to look over their mills, paper and cotton, also their ice factory, at a place called Mundwha, about 4 miles away. The girls went with some of the younger members of the Pudumjie family and I drove with some elders. They had tea and all sorts of refreshments at the mills office for us after our inspection.

Young Arthur came to dinner to help to eat his hare, which was very good.

OCT 25 I went for a drive in the evening with Arthur in the dummy, to call on Sir A. Hunter and General Richardson.

OCT 26 Georgie, Helen and I went to an "At Home" at the Council Hall given by members of the National Indian Association. Many Parsees, Brahmins and Mahomedans present. Arthur dined at the Club of Western India with Colonel Channer.

OCT 29 Dined with Sir Archibald Hunter. I didn't want to go as Arthur was away but, as he wished it. I had to go. Very lively, informal entertainment.

OCT 30 Arthur and Arthur T. got back about 2.30 p.m. bringing a deer shot by the latter.

NOV 1 Much packing!

NOV 2 Directly we were dressed we all helped to move things from the house to the tents pitched under some trees in the compound, about 200 yards away. By breakfast time, which we had in the big tent we have hired, everything was quite ready and comfortable.

So, here we are, until we find it convenient to move.

Directly after breakfast Helen went off to Kirkee for a few days with the Jooks'. I am very glad, for her sake, that she has this little change and it is just as well to be without her bulky presence for a day or two!

NOV 3 Colonel Channer came early to say good bye pro tem for, at a special hunt meeting last night, Arthur was begged to return and hunt here next season, offering extra advantages, which he accepted.

Colonel Channer knew I should not be pleased, personally, so teased me by offering sympathy etc., chuckling with delight at the thought of getting Arthur back, all the time! Gertie Channer came over in the evening for good byes.

NOV 4 I took the little ones to a lovely party given by Major Bertie Clay (inventor of the Dum Dum ballet) where they ran races and got boxes of chocolates and heaps of crackers, afterwards going on to see fireworks and the burning of a gigantic "Guy". Mrs Jooks brought her children and Helen with them, we didn't get back to camp till 8.30 p.m.

NOV 5 Early visit from Colonel Bull who also goes to Bombay this evening for duties connected with the Royal visit.

NOV 13 I went to the station to see Arthur off to Bombay.

At the last I had to give up. For all the arrangements we tried to make for getting to the Ball given tonight in honour of the Prince and Princess of Wales fell through! Arthur has gone to stay in camp with Arthur T. for a couple of nights. So he is all right. After tea I went for a long drive with Mrs Trevor and afterwards called in at the Gymkhana for Georgie, who had been playing tennis.

NOV 15 Arthur returned from Bombay. The little ones went alone, in the dummy, to the station to meet him.

NOV 16 Georgie, I and the babes, went for a long walk before breakfast by the canal. To their great delight I allowed the chicks to bathe in an off shoot of the canal where they splashed and floundered, for about a quarter of an hour, to their hearts' joy!

NOV 17 Arthur and I played croquet at Gymkhana before breakfast.

DEC 7 A long time since I made an entry. All plans for going home were suddenly knocked on the head by Helen developing enteric whilst staying at Kirkee. She went to the Sassoon Hospital on Nov 21. and after being very ill for a week, gradually improved on Dec 4. Colonel Burke hopes she will be able to travel by the end of the month.

General and Mrs Richardson, with goodness unbounded, took us all in on Nov 24 and here we are still, for they are so extremely generous and kind as to say we are to stay until we can sail.

DEC 23 General and Mrs Richardson, with their nephew (and ADC) Captain Gordon, left yesterday for a ten days Christmas outing with the Rajah of Bikanir. They pressed us to stay and make use of their house and servants to the last, but as Helen is now quite out of the wood we thought we would spend a week in Bombay. Accordingly, Arthur and I, with the two little ones and Shiwa, went by 11 o'clock train, a very slow one, and reached our hotel, the Great Western, about 6.30 p.m.

DEC 24 Went in the morning to see our boat, the Massilia, and found Mr Robertson, the Purser and Mr McKay, the Chief Engineer, the same men who had been in similar positions on the Asia when we came out nearly five years ago.

DEC 25 Christmas Day. We spent it at Palli Hill with the Pikes.

DEC 26 Arthur and I spent nearly all the morning going round the Bombay Stables Company's premises, seeing hundreds of horses; Australians, Arabs, Persian and Hungarian, in various stages of education.

DEC 28 I went to the shipping office for tickets and to various banks connected with home coming. I forgot to say that before doing this we had a capital swim in the swimming bath which can be engaged at certain times for families and which Arthur had, accordingly, taken. The little ones were very plucky although at the shallow end of the bath there were four feet of water.

DEC 29 Colonel Bull and Mr Pike came to lunch with us after which I took the little ones to Jackie Pike's Christmas Tree.

Spent the whole morning with the children in the Victoria Gardens, Bombay's Zoo, to their infinite satisfaction.

DEC 30 Did a hard day's work, packing and giving a final scrub to my own and the children's hair.

DEC 31 Directly breakfast was over Arthur went to the station to meet Georgie and Helen and I took the little ones to the ship, to which we had also sent Shiwa forward with the luggage. Before Arthur arrived with the girls and young Arthur, who joined them on the journey, I had got our luggage all comfortably stowed away in our respective cabins. Helen arrived, looking pale, but otherwise quite herself. Georgie and Arthur very bright and well.

At 11 a.m. all passengers had to go ashore for plague inspection and, soon after this, "friends of passengers" had to leave the ship. For some time we carried on a shouting conversation with Georgie and Arthur jr., from the ship's side to the dock, where they were standing and soon after 12 noon we gradually moved away.

Directly we got out of dock we had the narrowest escape of being run into by a huge P & O boat, which, contrary to every nautical rule, ran clean across our bows. Nothing but the very smart precision of our captain in dropping his anchor saved us from a collision which, the captain said, would probably have sunk both ships.

JAN 3 1906 Actually, I have not been sick and this is the fourth day at sea. There are very few passengers and we have two roomy and extremely cool cabins, on the starboard side of the ship. The sea has been very smooth and the ship as steady as possible, there seems less motion than in a train and it is so cool that I am glad to wear a light coat over my thin Indian clothes nearly all day.

JAN 12 Friday. We reached Suez at a quarter to seven this morning after a somewhat slow and monotonous, but an exceptionally good, passage. The weather has been perfect and the ship marvellously steady. No-one has been sea-sick, not even me! Though I was clean knocked over for a day and a half with a most abominable headache and could not sit up at all. I found the luxury of travelling for the first time with a maid! (Helen) who relieved me of all duties with the little ones.

Our fellow passengers are all very uninteresting and, I dare say, the Sheringham family strike them in much the same light.

I am writing at 2 p.m. and we ought to have started down the canal an hour and a half ago but a big boat, outward bound, has twice got a-ground. They have just got her afloat with steam tugs and we can see her rounding the last bend so I suppose we shall soon get away. The captain said, at lunch, that if we had to wait until night he would get a steam launch and take us all ashore.

JAN 19 We left Suez at 3 p.m. on the 12th and made a clean run through the canal, not meeting a single ship. We reached Port Said at 4.30 a.m. and coaling by electric light began at once.

The coal dust soon smothered everything and everybody so, as soon as we were dressed Arthur and I, with Helen and the babes, went ashore. We were amused looking into shop windows, buying English newspapers, and generally "loafing" about. We took the children for a run on the sands at the back of Lesseps' statue and they picked up heaps of shells. We returned to the Massilia about 9.30. Leaving Port Said we had a peaceful afternoon in the Mediterranian, the wind, however, got up in the night and in the early morning I knew, by my

giddy, aching, head, that I had been tossed about for some hours.
Whilst having my bath sea-sickness began and I hastily stumbled back to my berth where I was thankful to spend the whole day. Baby next succumbed but recovered after a little sickness and a good sleep. Next, Ruth had to give in and remained in her berth, but Helen and Arthur kept quite well.

The morning of the 15th was much smoother and gradually the next day improved. I also got out heaps of warm clothing and in the snug embrace of my elderly fur cloak I spent quite a comfortable day on deck. The 16th was a wild day; seas mountains high but with a following wind the motion was not bad. The chief trial was the pouring rain which continued incessantly, from dawn until 5 p.m., quite preventing any airing on deck. The saloon, with doors and ports shut, became intollerably stuffy and the children (there are seven or eight besides ours) got quarrelsome and generally disagreeable. However, when the rain cleared, we had a good blow on deck before tubbing them and putting them to bed.

The 17th and 18th were cold, fresh days with delightfully smooth sea and bright sun. We came through the Straits of Messina early on the 17th and a few hours after passed Stromboli, thence taking a Northerly course to the North of Corsica, instead of through the Straits of Bonifacio, as we did in the Britannia, in 1903.

JAN 19 Bitterly cold wind with rather a choppy sea but bright sun and exquisite views of the French coast, with snow clad Alps in the background. Reached Marseilles and had to wait a little time in quarantine until the Dr. came aboard to pass us free of sickness.

Next came the pilot and we were in dock just before dark, about 5.30 p.m. The various people direct for London left the Massilia almost at once and the rest of us had a delightfully quiet night in the dock.

JAN 24 We got away just before daylight failed. We had quite a jolly little visit in Marseilles where the weather, although bitterly cold was exquisitely clear and bright. One day Arthur and I went by train as far into the country as it would take us. Then we walked five or six miles further, through vineyards and orchards and up some very steep, rough hills, where we had a lovely view. We refreshed ourselves at a village restaurant and didn't get back to the ship until nearly 6 p.m.

having started at 10 in the morning.
At other times we made various jaunts into town for shopping, a visit to a Music Hall matinee and occasional cups of "cafe au lait" in the pavement restaurants. These things made up the sum of our amusements.

JAN 25 As soon as we were clear of Marseilles harbour yesterday we got into choppy sea which quickly grew worse owing to a gale which sprung up. The ship being now very much lighter, having discharged heavy cargo at Marseilles and taken on much lighter goods in the shape of hides, cork, cedar wood, wines, oil and soap, behaved like a baby, bobbing, rolling, pitching and lurching. So, directly I had given the little ones their tub at 6 p.m., I rolled myself in all sorts of warm night clothing and tumbled into bed. I had a cup of Bovril, instead of any dinner and slept most of the night waking only now and again when the ship gave an extra big lurch, or the wind an extra loud howl. Helen and the little ones did the same and this morning things are decidedly better; the sun is bright and the air warmer. The sea too, though not quite as calm as I could wish, leaves the ship fairly steady and more improvement may be safely anticipated, at any rate until we reach Gib.

JAN 27 Anchored outside Gibralter this morning, about 9 a.m. The night had been quite hot and, remembering the temperature of "The Rock" last time I was there, I made great reductions in my own, and the children's clothing. Everyone went ashore directly after breakfast and when we had walked quite a short distance down the Main Street I was saluted by a young giant, in uniform, but with the rosy, smiling face of Ivan Newton, for whom we were prepared as we had sent word to him that we were coming.

We went first to the Calpe Kennels and saw the hounds, 40 couple, in first rate condition. In course of conversation with the kennel man he told me that the hounds had not been out regularly lately as "that had been so dry." This unmistakable Norfolkism made me ask what county he came from and he at once replied, "I live at Saham, nare Watton, not fer from Naradge." This brought me nearer home than I have been for 2 1/2 years.

We spent the rest of our time wandering round to a primitive little

fishing village called Catalan, quite under the highest part of the Rock. The children picked up shells on the beach and we gradually worked our way back to the quay.
We said good-bye here to Ivan and got back to the Massilia a little before 2 p.m. By 3 p.m. we had started for our last bit of the voyage, with the addition of two passengers, a man and a lady, and some more cargo in the shape of cork and feathers!

. . . .

This was the last entry in the diary bringing to a close, on the 25th January, 1906, a record begun on 1st May, 1901.

The Diarist in later years

Biography

Rachel Anna Sheringham (nee Garland), born 25.1.1858 died 9.11.1945.
Less is known about Rachel Anna than of her second husband, Colonel Arthur William Sheringham. Her place of birth is not known, in fact all we know of her early years is that she was at school at Bognor. At the time of writing the diary her mother was living in Chester but there is no reason to suppose that she came from there. It may be no more than a coincidence that Arthur served for five years as Commander of the Cheshire Regiment.

Rachel's first marriage was to William George Sheringham, a wool, wine and seed merchant of Fakenham, Norfolk. They were married on 5th August 1880 and lived at 2, Market Square, Fakenham, Woolworths now occupy the site. There were seven children of the marriage, six daughters and a son. Her husband, William, died on 26th February 1896 aged 41 years.

The following year, on the 20th April, Rachel married William's cousin, Arthur. At the time of the marriage Arthur had recently taken command of the 22nd Regimental District. Where he was stationed is not known.

There were two children of Rachel's second marriage, Ruth, born on 22nd February 1898 and Rachel, born on 7th June 1900.

In the diary Rachel mentions sea voyages she had made prior to the journey to India. These may have been during her first marriage as it is known that the Sheringhams had relatives in Virginia. Arthur retired from the army in 1901 after many years service overseas, principally in India judging by his evident attachment to that country.

Following the death of Arthur in November 1923 Rachel moved, with her two daughters, to Rustington, in Sussex. Rachel's declining years were spent in the nurses home in Weybridge where Georgina, her eldest step-daughter, also lived, Georgina being a nurse in the Queen Alexandra's Royal Army Nursing Corps. Rachel died on the 9th November 1945 at the age of 87 years.

Muriel Cross Mary Herdman Ruth Sheringham

Rachel Sheringham

Postcript

The diary ends, abruptly. All knowledge of the family is lost to us until in 1977, an article appeared in a publication devoted to the history of Caston, Norfolk, written by Miss Ruth Sheringham and her younger sister Rachel. The article told how they returned with their parents in 1906, father having bought Flaxmoor, a house in Caston. Ruth told how they loved living there and how, after more than fifty years, they still thought of it as "home".

In June 1911 disaster struck the family; with the failure of the Charing Cross Bank all their savings were lost and they were obliged to let their home. Colonel Sheringham and his wife had never been ones to allow themselves to be overcome by adversity and later in the year the family departed for Virginia where they stayed with relatives until returning to Flaxmoor in 1913. Their style of life does not appear to have been greatly altered and one is left to suppose that during the two years in America the family managed to recover from the loss of their investments.

While staying with her Aunt Alice in Virginia Ruth rode with Tom Mix, the star of several Western films. (In 1925 Tom Mix, and his horse, "Tony", came to England as the guests of the Lord Mayor of London).

Leaving school in 1916 Ruth worked as a land worker before joining the W.R.A.F. in 1917 as a driver. After demobilisation she had the first motor cycle in Caston and acted as chauffeur to a doctor from Watton. A year after writing the article Ruth's sister, Rachel, died. She followed her less than four months later. Among her effects was found a business card announcing that, shortly after the Great War, Ruth had taken over a riding school in Buckingham Palace Road. To supplement her income she specialised in retraining horses which had returned from war service.

Colonel Arthur Sheringham had his leg amputated in 1921, at the age of 77. However this did not deter him from continuing to hunt game. In order to do this he had a revolving office chair nailed to a donkey cart! He died, aged 79, in 1923.

Ilex, who is mentioned on the first page of the diary, was named after a race horse. He joined the Ceylon Police and never returned to England. Arthur junior became a Major in the Indian Army and was awarded the D.S.O. Georgina was a nurse serving in India with the Queen Alexandra's Royal Army Nursing Corps from the beginning of the century. She devoted her life to the Q.A.s' and did not marry.

Sadly, Helen died at the age of 26, in 1917 and is buried next to her father in Caston churchyard.